BRAIN GAMES

CRIMINAL MIND PUZZLES

Publications International, Ltd.

Puzzle creators: Myles Callum, Andrew Clarke, Caroline Delbert, Adrian Fisher, David Millar, Stephen Ryder, Nicole Sulgit

Puzzle illustrators: Eric Biel, Caroline Delbert, Chris Gattorna, Eddy Mirko, Lou Newton, Stephanie Rocha, Brent Saemann, Shavan R. Spears, Jen Torche, Kelsey Waitkus

Additional images from Shutterstock.com

Louis Weber, CEO
Publications International, Ltd.
8140 Lehigh Avenue
Morton Grove, IL 60053

ISBN: 978-1-64030-673-8

Manufactured in China.

8 7 6 5 4 3 2 1

TIME TO DETECT

Are you a true crime buff? Do you watch detectives on TV and think you could solve the crime in less time? Now you can test your investigative prowess with *Brain Games®: Criminal Mind Puzzles*. Here, you'll find numerous crime-themed puzzles that will challenge your visual, verbal, memory, and logical skills.

"Seen at the Scene" puzzles ask you to spot small details of crime scenes, while "Overheard Information" puzzles test your memory. "Crack the Password" puzzles ask you to unscramble the criminal's passwords, while "Interception" puzzles push you to decode an intercepted message. With "Find the Witness" and "Motel Hideout" puzzles, you'll have to use your logical skills. Throughout the book, you'll solve puzzles themed around art thefts, bank robbery, and murder. You'll solve some puzzles with bursts of inspiration, while others will require hard word as you track down a chain of logic.

Don't worry if you find yourself getting stuck from time to time. Answers are located at the back of the book when you need a helpful boost.

Are you ready to test alibis, solve crimes, and track down criminals? Just open the book to any page and start solving!

A FAMOUS CRIME

Cryptograms are messages in substitution code. Break the code to read the message. For example, THE SMART CAT might become FVO QWGDF JGF if **F** is substituted for **T**, **V** for **H**, **O** for **E**, and so on.

1994 RVW SBF SBFAS LA V UFPRCLI LA FKUVPK
HTINB'R MVCISCIJ SBF RNPFVH APLH V JVGGFPY
CI LRGL. SBF SBCFUFR GFAS QFBCIK V ILSF SBVIECIJ
SBF HTRFTH ALP MLLP RFNTPCSY. SBF GVRS GVTJB
WVR LI SBF HTRFTH, SBLTJB, VR MLGCNF PFNLUFPFK
SBF MVCISCIJ VIK NVTJBS SBF SBCFUFR.

INTERCEPTION

You've intercepted a message. You think it might be the location of a meeting between two criminals, but it doesn't seem to make sense. Can you decipher the true message?

**WILL SKIING HUBBLE BURR BAA PURR YAY
IMMUNE SOON INNS MEDDLE AARDWOLF YUCKY.**

Answers on page 175.

WHAT CHANGED? PART I

Study this picture of the crime scene for 1 minute, then turn the page.

WHAT CHANGED? PART II

(Do not read this until you have read the previous page!)
From memory, can you tell what changed between this page and the previous page?

Answers on page 175.

FIND THE WITNESS

On Riverdell Street, there are 5 houses. You need to follow up with a witness, Harriet Chin, but without any address on the doors you are not sure which house to approach. You know from the previous interview that Chin is a single mother with a daughter. The staff at the corner bakery and your own observations give you some clues. From the information given, can you find the right house?

A. The two corner houses are green, while the others are blue. There is a child or children living in one green house and two blue houses.

B. An elderly widower lives alone in the middle house.

C. The nanny for the couple in house E regularly brings her charge by for a treat at the bakery.

D. Sometimes she brings in the daughter of her next door neighbor, but the nanny doesn't like the boy further down the street.

House A   House B   House C   House D   House E

Answers on page 175.

TEST THE ALIBI

Detectives are investigating a murder. The victim, Michael Jones, left dinner with his friends at 6 PM and took a rideshare home. The rideshare driver swiped his credit card at 6:37 PM and saw Jones enter his house. Jones was discovered dead by his sister, who rented his second floor, at approximately 11 PM.

The prime suspect, Kristen Brightly, claims that she was at a large work function and company party, followed by dinner and drinks with friends. Because she was about a 20-minute drive away from the crime scene, the detectives are trying to see if there is a time window of about one hour when she could have committed the murder. From the following witness statements, can you verify the alibi?

Rideshare drivers were able to corroborate the following:

Brightly was picked up outside her workplace at 7:50 PM and dropped off outside the restaurant where she was to meet her friends at 8:10 PM.

Brightly and a friend were picked up outside the restaurant at 10:30 PM and dropped off outside another nearby bar at 10:40 PM.

Brightly's colleagues attested to the following:

Brightly gave the last speech of the function at 4:30 PM.

One colleague tracked her down at the end of the evening, around 7:30 PM, to tell her it had been a good speech.

Two colleagues had a conversation with her while eating snacks after her speech. They know it was around 6 because a clock bell rang during their conversation, and estimate they talked with her for anywhere between 10 and 20 minutes after that.

A colleague saw her in the bathroom at one point, but couldn't narrow the time further than "sometime before 6 PM."

Other colleagues also remembered her being at the function, but couldn't give specific times beyond, "shortly after her speech" or "later in the evening."

Her friends and restaurant staff attested to the following:

Brightly and her friends had scheduled to meet at 8:30 PM. Brightly was the first to arrive and told the host that she would wait on the bench outside, as the weather was nice, rather than at the bar. The group was seated shortly after 8:30 PM.

Four friends attested to Brightly being there with them until 10:30 PM, and never leaving beyond a few minutes to go to the bathroom or take a phone call. Restaurant staff remember the group being there without anyone leaving, and credit card receipts attest that they paid and left around 10:30 PM.

Answers on page 175.

SEEN AT THE SCENE PART I

Study this picture of the crime scene for 1 minute, then turn the page.

SEEN AT THE SCENE PART II

(Do not read this until you have read the previous page!)
Which image exactly matches the picture from the previous page?

1.

2.

3.

4.

Answers on page 175.

WEDDING BELL BLUES PART I

Read this true crime account, then turn to the next page to test your knowledge.

Undercover FBI agents spent several years watching their targets—members of an international counterfeiting and smuggling ring—and developing a relationship with them. It worked so well that the ultimate wedding sting operation just fell into place.

Two of the agents, who had gained the trust of the criminals, posed as bride and groom, with a fake wedding that was months in the making. A date was set, and invitations were sent out. The wedding was planned for 2 P.M. on a Sunday afternoon in August 2005, just off the coast of New Jersey. A luxury yacht named *Operation Royal Charm* was docked outside of Atlantic City, and guests started arriving from far and wide. No detail was forgotten: Guests and the bridal party were decked out in wedding finery befitting the high rollers that they were. There were even wedding presents, including a pair of Presidential Rolex watches.

But when the guests boarded a boat that they thought would take them out to the yacht, they got a bit of a surprise. There was no wedding! And instead of a cruise on a luxury boat, eight wedding guests got caught in an FBI sting that led to the arrest of about 60 other residents of Asia and the United States, all involved in a variety of international trafficking crimes.

Authorities seized $4.4 million in counterfeit $100 bills, $42 million worth of counterfeit cigarettes, $700,000 worth of fake U.S. postage stamps and blue jeans, and very real quantities of Viagra, ecstasy, and methamphetamine. The criminals were also charged with conspiracy to ship $1 million of automatic rifles, silenced pistols, submachine guns, and rocket launchers—none of which were delivered.

WEDDING BELL BLUES PART II

(Do not read this until you have read the previous page!)

1. What year did the fake wedding take place?
A. 2002
B. 2003
C. 2004
D. 2005

2. What was the name of the yacht used in the bust?
A. Operation Royal Charm
B. Operation Wedding Bells
C. Charm Royale
D. Wedding Charm

3. How much in counterfeit money was seized?
A. $42 million
B. $4.4 million
C. $1 million
D. $700,000

4. The boat was docked outside this city.
A. New York City
B. Savannah
C. Atlantic City
D. Boston

Answers on page 175.

TREASURE HUNT

The investigator is tracking a jewelry thief's past trips in order to find and recover jewelry that was left behind in six cities. Each city was visited only once. Can you put together the travel timeline, using the information below?

1. Mexico City was either the first or last city.

2. From Toronto, the thief went directly to Tulsa.

3. The trip to Cleveland took place sometime before the trip to Houston, but not immediately before.

4. After almost being caught in Las Vegas, the thief fled the United States for a while before returning to a U.S. city.

5. The thief visited Ohio directly before Nevada.

6. From Houston, the thief traveled south to the next city on the trip.

Answers on page 176.

MOTEL HIDEOUT

A thief hides out in one of the 45 motel rooms listed in the chart below. The motel's in-house detective received a sheet of four clues, signed "The Logical Thief." Using these clues, the detective found the room number within 15 minutes—but by that time, the thief had fled. Can you find the thief's motel room more quickly?

1. Neither digit is 3.

2. The sum of the digits is either 5, 7, or 10.

3. If the digits were flipped, the resulting number would be found on the chart.

4. The number is prime.

51	52	53	54	55	56	57	58	59
41	42	43	44	45	46	47	48	49
31	32	33	34	35	36	37	38	39
21	22	23	24	25	26	27	28	29
11	12	13	14	15	16	17	18	19

Answers on page 176.

SEEN AT THE SCENE PART I

Study this picture of the crime scene for 1 minute, then turn the page.

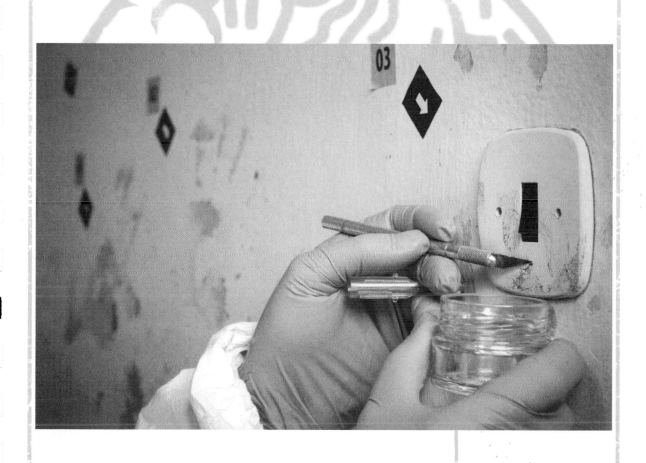

SEEN AT THE SCENE PART II

(Do not read this until you have read the previous page!)
Which image exactly matches the picture from the previous page?

1.

2.

3.

4.

Answers on page 176.

OVERHEARD INFORMATION PART I

Read the story below, then turn the page and answer the questions.

While on a train, a bystander overheard a conversation between two thieves about where some stolen money and goods were stashed. The man said, "Okay, the police are keeping an eye out for me in that area, so I can't make it to the Parkway house. Don't be seen on Parkway—go to the house that backs up to it on Warden Drive and go through the tunnel. The cash is in the safe. Take out $5,000 and leave the rest there. Combination is 08-65-12, August-Medicare-December. The phones are in the attic in the cedar chest."

OVERHEARD INFORMATION PART II

(Do not read this until you have read the previous page!)

1. The accomplice is directed to take this much money from the safe.

A. Half of the $5,000 found there.

B. $5,000, which is half of what is found there

C. $5,000, which is an unspecified portion of what is found there

D. $5,000, the total sum found there

2. The house containing the safe and goods is found on this street.

A. Parkway

B. Parkland

C. Warden

D. Wardway

3. The mnemonic the thief provides for the safe combination is this.

A. Octogon-Medicare-Christmas

B. August-Medicare-December

C. August-Medicare-Christmas

D. August-December-Medicare

4. The phones are found here.

A. A cedar chest

B. The basement

C. The living room

D. The safe

Answers on page 176.

CRIME RHYMES

Each clue leads to a 2-word answer that rhymes, such as BIG PIG or STABLE TABLE. The numbers in parentheses after the clue give the number of letters in each word. For example, "cookware taken from the oven (3, 3)" would be "hot pot."

1. When investigators are weighing whether to charge someone with a crime, it is said that they (5, 6): _____

2. The burglar who stole food from a variety of summer picnickers was known as the (10, 5): _____

3. The doctor who thought his patient was being poisoned could be said to have a (9, 9): _____

4. The detective who like this sweet wine was known as the (8, 6): _____

5. When the criminal left traces of an adhesive at the scene, it was known as the (4, 4): _____

6. When the captain's second in command seemed suspicious, the detective chose to (11, 5, 4): _____ (the) _____ _____

7. A murder next to a body of water (8, 8): _____

8. A person who wants to be an investigator (11, 9): _____

CRIME ON TV

ACROSS

1. Aptly named forensics crime show on Fox
6. Milkmaid's needs
11. Byron or Keats
12. In ___ (agitated)
13. City visited by pilgrims
14. Beauty pageant crown
15. Ailing chemistry teacher turns to crime (AMC)
17. Leonardo ___, a.k.a. Fibonacci
18. They tempted Ulysses
21. "Bravo, torero!"
24. Captain in "The Caine Mutiny"
25. Cool red giant in the sky
27. Range of sizes, briefly
28. Donny or Marie, by birth
29. "8 Mile" rapper
32. Dark yet funny TBS mystery starring Alia Shawkat
37. "Who's there?" reply, perhaps
38. Bolivian city, former capital
39. Oscar actress Garson
40. Go ballistic, with "out"
41. Avian abodes
42. Dark-comedy crime drama with Billy Bob Thornton as a hitman in Minnesota (FX)

DOWN

1. Big flop
2. German/Czech river
3. "Good work!"
4. Object of a manhunt
5. Supporting, as tomato plants
6. City on the Ganges (or Lord Jim's ship)
7. Not ___ of (no trace of)
8. Where diner patrons may prefer to sit
9. Former Italian money
10. End of many Dutch town names
16. NASA orbiter
18. Four-sided figs.
19. Chemical suffix.
20. Puts out, as a record
22. Anaheim baseball team, in box scores
23. Fish-catching eagle
25. Debark
26. John O'Hara's "Appointment in ___"
28. The Wildcats of the NCAA, for short
30. Shea Stadium mascot
31. Cake decorators
32. Communicate by hand
33. Being, in Paris
34. One who's sorry
35. "King Lear" or "Hamlet": Abbr.
36. Lennon's wife

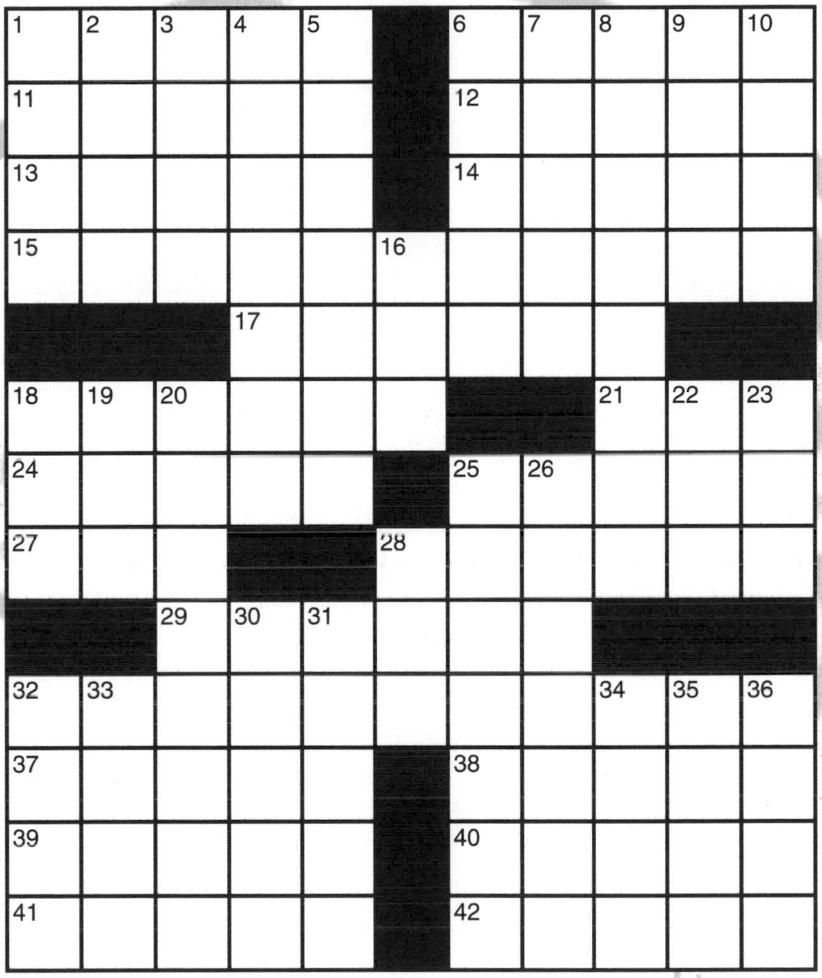

Answers on page 176.

SPOTTING A CLUE

Change just one letter on each line to go from the top word to the bottom word. Do not change the order of the letters. You must have an English word at each step.

SPOT

_____

_____

_____ to turn or skid

CLUE

FORGING MONEY

Change just one letter on each line to go from the top word to the bottom word. Do not change the order of the letters. You must have an English word at each step.

FORGE

_____

_____

_____ things in a front position or golfer's warnings

_____

_____

_____

MONEY

Answers on page 177.

SEEN AT THE SCENE PART I

Study this picture of the crime scene for 1 minute, then turn the page.

SEEN AT THE SCENE PART II

(Do not read this until you have read the previous page!)
Which image exactly matches the picture from the previous page?

1.

2.

3.

4.

Answers on page 177.

FIND THE WITNESS

There are 5 houses on Parson Avenue. You need to follow up with a witness, Danny Boyd, but the paperwork only lists his street, not his specific address. You know from the previous interview that Boyd lives with his girlfriend, and Boyd drives a motorcycle. The staff at the corner bakery and your own observations give you some clues. From the information given, can you find the right house?

A. Couples live in houses A, C, and D.

B. The worker at the bakery counter knows Boyd lives next to widow, because she used to complain about the noise of Boyd's motorcycle, but now she appreciates that Boyd clears her driveway of snow.

C. The bakery counter worker doesn't know which house the widow lives in, but she adds that the widow doesn't think as highly of the neighbor who lives on the other side of her.

D. Boyd's girlfriend was visiting the couple next door on the day he witnessed the crime.

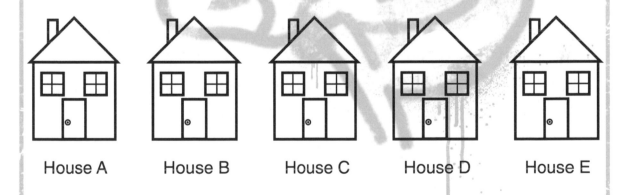

House A   House B   House C   House D   House E

Answers on page 177.

INTERCEPTION

You've intercepted a message that is meant to reveal a location for an upcoming meeting between two criminal masterminds. The only problem is, the message doesn't make much sense. Can you figure out the right location?

FIR ILIAD AWAY
NOVO OVEN
AUGUST LAURA NEXT A

WE STILL DON'T KNOW WHO DONE IT

Cryptograms are messages in substitution code. Break the code to read the message. For example, THE SMART CAT might become FVO QWGDF JGF if **F** is substituted for **T**, **V** for **H**, **O** for **E**, and so on.

DBQ OYIDPL PBLDARQS UYLQ GBRDARQL NKQONL DO YJNTDJC OJDI NKQ GLYWQAAY LNQTYJN MYJNBQJ IPLQPI. GB 1990, IQB FDLGBM YL FDAGUQ DOOGUQJL LNDAQ 13 TDJCL DO YJN TDJNK KPBSJQSL DO IGAAGDBL DO SDAAYJL. QIFNX OJYIQL YN NKQ IPLQPI LKDT TKQJQ NKQ YJNTDJC TYL.

MOTEL HIDEOUT

A thief hides out in one of the 45 motel rooms listed in the chart below. The motel's in-house detective received a sheet of four clues, signed "The Logical Thief." Using these clues, the detective found the room number within 15 minutes—but by that time, the thief had fled. Can you find the thief's motel room more quickly?

1. **The number is prime.**

2. **The first digit is not 2 or a multiple of 2.**

3. **If you flipped the digits, the resulting number would be less than 50.**

4. **The sum of the digits is less than 4.**

51	52	53	54	55	56	57	58	59
41	42	43	44	45	46	47	48	49
31	32	33	34	35	36	37	38	39
21	22	23	24	25	26	27	28	29
11	12	13	14	15	16	17	18	19

Answers on page 177.

BOTCHED CRIME JOBS PART I

Read these true crime accounts, then turn to page 30 to test your knowledge.

Not everything goes off without a hitch. In fact, it rarely does. Here are some examples of some of the most-botched crime jobs in history.

1. Organized crime is serious business. After all, it usually involves violence, weapons, other people's money, the law, and prison. With those pieces loose on the chessboard, it's really easy to mess up. Take the two New York mobsters who agreed to do a little job: hit Al Capone. They had a nice trip on the Twentieth Century Limited, but in Chicago they were met at the train, taken someplace quiet, and beaten to death. Pieces of them were sent back with a note: "Don't send boys to do a man's job."

2. There's also the mistake of not knowing who you're dealing with. Faced with debts in his electrical business, Florida businessperson George Bynum borrowed $50,000 from a mob loan shark. He was able to make $2,500 payments on the interest, but he couldn't pay off the principal, so he decided to go into the crime business himself. He tipped off a burglary gang about a house that he had wired, in exchange for a cut of the take. The burglars broke in, but the home owner was there, and they beat him up. The owner was Anthony "Nino" Gaggi, a Gambino family mobster.

Gaggi found out that Bynum had planned the burglary. On July 13, 1976, John Holland called Bynum from the Ocean Shore Motel and pitched a lucrative wiring contract. When Bynum arrived at the motel, Gaggi and some friends were waiting, and that was the last anyone heard from Bynum.

3. Often the bungling of criminals is much more humorous. Enrico "Kiko" Frigerio was a Swiss citizen, and when the famed Pizza Connection—a scheme to push heroin through pizza parlors in New York—was broken by the FBI in 1984, he fled to Switzerland. Frigerio stayed there for years, until a documentary film crew decided to do a movie about his life. As technical advisor, he decided to give them a tour of his old New York haunts, but when he stepped off a plane onto U.S. soil, he was immediately arrested. Frigerio hadn't realized that he was still under indictment. Oops!

4. Jimmy Breslin once wrote a comic novel called *The Gang That Couldn't Shoot Straight.* He must have been thinking about New Jersey's DeCavalcante crime family, the only one never given a seat on the Mafia's ruling commission. Vincent "Vinnie Ocean" Palermo ruled the DeCavalcante family like a bad Marx Brothers movie. Once, Palermo's men were given a supply of free cell phones—supplied by the FBI to tap their conversations. Another time, Palermo put a .357 Magnum to the head of a boat mechanic to force him to admit that he'd ruined the motor on Palermo's speedboat. "I was so mad, I bit his nose," Palermo said.

Then there was the time that Palermo and the missus went on vacation, and he decided to hide the family jewelry—$700,000 worth—in the bottom of a trash bag. "My wife took the garbage out for the first time in 20 years, and that was the end of the jewelry."

Finally, in 1999, Palermo was arrested and agreed to turn informant in exchange for leniency in sentencing. He helped to put away such stalwarts as Frankie the Beast, Anthony Soft-Shoes, and Frank the Painter. Palermo himself admitted to four murders, including that of newspaper editor Frank Weiss. He said that it was a good career move: "I shot him twice in the head. They made me a captain." He will not be missed.

BOTCHED CRIME JOBS PART II

(Do not read this until you have read the previous page!)

1. Which gangster sent the mobster who ordered a hit on him the note, "Don't send boys to do a man's job"?
A. Al Capone
B. Anthony Gaggi
C. Enrico Frigerio
D. Vinnie Palermo

2. Anthony Gaggi belonged to this crime family.
A. Ninos
B. Gambinos
C. Palermos
D. DeCavalcantes

3. Who was caught because he returned to the U.S. from Switzerland in order to help a film crew?
A. Al Capone
B. George Bynum
C. Enrico Frigerio
D. Vincent Palermo

4. Palermo's wife accidentally put this much jewelry in the trash.
A. $100,000
B. $250,000
C. $500,000
D. $700,000

Answers on page 177.

SEEN AT THE SCENE PART I

Study this picture of the crime scene for 1 minute, then turn the page.

SEEN AT THE SCENE PART II

(Do not read this until you have read the previous page!)
Which image exactly matches the picture from the previous page?

1.

2.

3.

4.

Answers on page 178.

TREASURE HUNT

The investigator is tracking a jewelry thief's past trips in order to find and recover jewelry that was left behind in six cities. Each city was visited only once. Can you put together the travel timeline, using the information below?

1. The thief did not go from Albany to Newark or vice versa.

2. The trip to Los Angeles took place after the trip to Toronto, but not immediately.

3. Madison was either the first or last location visited.

4. From Dallas the thief fled directly to Newark.

5. The thief did not begin in a province or state that borders a Great Lake.

Answers on page 178.

FINGERPRINT MATCH

Find the matching fingerprint(s). There may be more than one.

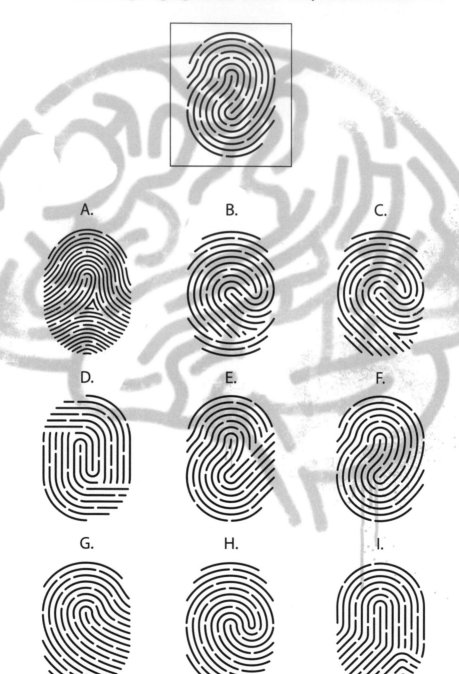

A.

B.

C.

D.

E.

F.

G.

H.

I.

Answers on page 178.

OVERHEARD INFORMATION PART I

Read the story below, then turn the page and answer the questions.

While on a train, a bystander overheard a criminal tell an accomplice about an upcoming set of crimes. The criminal said, "We don't need you for the hit on the grocery store on the 20th, but we need a getaway driver for the next day. We're going back to that music store on Pearson Street, you know the one. And then we're going to that little diner on Fourth Street next weekend while our mutual friend is bussing tables so he can help us out."

OVERHEARD INFORMATION PART II

(Do not read this until you have read the previous page!)

The bystander overheard the information about the crimes that were planned, but didn't have anywhere to write it down! Answer the questions below to help the bystander remember what to tell the police.

1. The hit on the music store will take place on this day.
A. The 20th
B. The 21st
C. Next weekend
D. A day is not specified.

2. The grocery store is found on this street.
A. Pearson Street
B. Fourth Street
C. Main Street
D. A location is not given.

3. The thief asks his accomplice to be a getaway driver for the hit on the grocery store.
A. True
B. False

4. The thieves will have a man on the inside at this location.
A. Grocery store
B. Music store
C. Diner
D. None of the above

Answers on page 178.

SEEN AT THE SCENE PART I

Study this picture of the crime scene for 1 minute, then turn the page.

SEEN AT THE SCENE PART II

(Do not read this until you have read the previous page!)
Which image exactly matches the picture from the previous page?

1.

2.

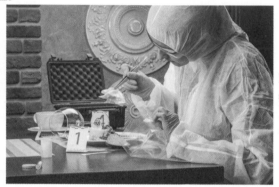

3.

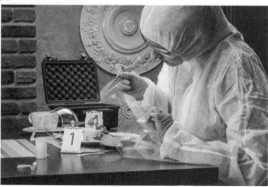

4.

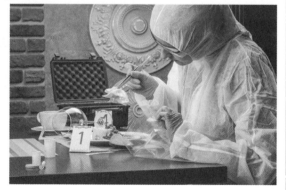

Answers on page 178.

GOING UNDERCOVER PART I

Read the story below, then turn the page and answer the questions.

You're an investigator going undercover in a grocery store that's believed to be a front for a counterfeiting and drug smuggling ring. Here are the people you're asked to investigate:

The owner, TJ Henson, is the brother of the suspected leader of the ring. He is 58 years old. He has done time for check forgery in his 30s. He is married to Brooke, who occasionally drops by the shop to arrange items in the flower section.

Brooke may or may not know about TJ's past and about his present alleged crimes. The couple has been married for ten years. Brooke has no priors, however, she has been seen in the store frequently on days that deliveries of drugs are believed to arrive. Brooke is 48.

TJ's brother, Wade, is the suspected leader of the ring. He has been convicted previously of drug trafficking. He is 61 years old. While only TJ's name is on the ownership documents for the store, employees are told that Wade is a silent partner, and to do what he says when he's around.

There are four full-time employees. Vernon Johnson, 45, is a suspected accomplice. It is believed that he makes deliveries of forged money and drugs for TJ and Wade. His official title is assistant manager. He has no criminal record.

Wanda Rove, 32, has been with the store since she was a teenager. It was her statements to a ex-boyfriend who later reported them to the police that triggered the investigation, wherein she said that her bosses had to be involved in shady things, but she kept her eyes firmly shut. She has no criminal record.

Eve Dawson, 18, has been a cashier and stocker for three months. She is not believed to be involved, although like Rove she may have been a witness to criminal dealings and chosen to turn a blind eye. She has no criminal record.

Leon Fuentes, 17, has been a stocker and bagger for eight months. He is TJ and Wade's nephew by their sister Rachel. It is believed that he has passed messages for the brothers, but it is not known whether he knew the contents of those messages or not. He has no criminal record.

GOING UNDERCOVER PART II

(Do not read this until you have read the previous page!)

1. Who is believed to be the leader of the ring?
A. TJ
B. Vernon
C. Brooke
D. Wade

2. Whose comments triggered the investigation?
A. Brooke
B. Eve
C. Wanda
D. Leon

3. Who served time for check forgery?
A. TJ
B. Wade
C. Vernon
D. Wanda

4. How long has Eve been with the store?
A. Three months
B. Eight months
C. Since she was a teenager
D. Unknown

Answers on page 178.

CRIME RHYMES

Each clue leads to a 2-word answer that rhymes, such as BIG PIG or STABLE TABLE. The numbers in parentheses after the clue give the number of letters in each word. For example, "cookware taken from the oven (3, 3)" would be "hot pot."

1. The case of the theft of the animal intestines was also called the case of the (6, 5): _____

2. A murder in December (8, 8): _____

3. The lawbreaker who sent hidden messages was the (10, 8): _____

4. To accuse a British "Sir" with a fancy title (6, 6): _____

5. A police inspector changes around assignments for the police under him (5, 4): _____

6. To take someone else's breakfast food (5, 7): _____

7. The smuggled dog was also called the (7, 6): _____

8. The incident of theft among the troupe of silent performers was called the (4, 5): _____

Answers on page 178.

NOTORIOUS ART THEFTS PART I

Read these true crime accounts, then turn to page 44 to test your knowledge.

Among the major robberies in the past hundred years are these daring thefts of very expensive art (values estimated at the time of the theft).

1. Boston, March 1990: $300 million

Two men dressed as police officers visited the Isabella Stewart Gardner Museum in the wee hours of the morning. After overpowering two guards and grabbing the security system's surveillance tape, they collected Rembrandt's only seascape, *Storm on the Sea of Galilee*, as well as Vermeer's *The Concert*, Manet's *Chez Tortoni*, and several other works. Authorities have yet to find the criminals despite investigating everyone from the Irish Republican Army to a Boston mob boss!

2. Oslo, August 2004: $120 million

Two armed and masked thieves threatened workers at the Munch Museum during a daring daylight theft. They stole a pair of Edvard Munch paintings, *The Scream* and *The Madonna*, estimated at a combined value of 100 million euros. In May 2006, authorities convicted three men who received between four and eight years in jail. The paintings were recovered three months later.

3. Paris, August 1911: $100 million

In the world's most notorious art theft to date, Vincenzo Peruggia, an employee of the Louvre, stole Leonardo da Vinci's *Mona Lisa* from the storied museum in the heart of Paris. Peruggia simply hid in a closet, grabbed the painting once alone in the room, hid it under his long smock, and walked out of the famed museum after it had closed. The theft turned the moderately popular *Mona Lisa* into the best-known painting in the world. Police questioned Pablo Picasso and French poet Guillaume Apollinaire about the crime, but they found the real thief—and the *Mona Lisa*—two years later when Peruggia tried to sell it to an art dealer in Florence.

4. Oslo, February 1994: $60-75 million

The Scream has been a popular target for thieves in Norway. On the day the 1994 Winter Olympics began in Lillehammer, a different version of Munch's famous work—he painted four—was taken from Oslo's National Art Museum. In less than one minute, the crooks came in through a window, cut the wires holding up the painting, and left through the same window. They attempted to ransom the painting to the Norwegian government, but they had left a piece of the frame at a bus stop—a clue that helped authorities recover the painting within a few months. Four men were convicted of the crime in January 1996.

5. Scotland, August 2003: $65 million

Blending in apparently has its advantages for art thieves. Two men joined a tour of Scotland's Drumlanrig Castle, subdued a guard, and made off with Leonardo da Vinci's *Madonna with the Yarnwinder*. Alarms around the art were not set during the day, and the thieves dissuaded tourists from intervening, reportedly telling them: "Don't worry...we're the police. This is just practice." Escaping in a white Volkswagen Golf, the perpetrators have never been identified—and the painting remains missing.

6. Stockholm, December 2000: $30 million

Caught! Eight criminals each got up to six and half years behind bars for conspiring to take a Rembrandt and two Renoirs—all of them eventually recovered—from Stockholm's National Museum. You have to give the three masked men who actually grabbed the paintings credit for a dramatic exit. In a scene reminiscent of an action movie, they fled the scene by motorboat. Police unraveled the plot after recovering one of the paintings during an unrelated drug investigation four months after the theft.

7. Amsterdam, December 2002: $30 million

Robbers used a ladder to get onto the roof of the Van Gogh Museum, then broke in and stole two of the Dutch master's paintings, *View of the Sea at Scheveningen* and *Congregation Leaving the Reformed Church in Nuenen*, together worth $30 million. Police told the press that the thieves worked so quickly that, despite setting off the museum's alarms, they had disappeared before police could get there. Authorities in the Netherlands arrested two men in 2003, based on DNA from hair inside two hats left at the scene, but they have been unable to recover the paintings, which the men deny taking.

NOTORIOUS ART THEFTS PART II

(Do not read this until you have read the previous page!)

1. Vincenzo Peruggia stole the *Mona Lisa* from this museum.
A. The Isabella Stewart Gardener
B. The Louvre
C. Oslo's National Art Museum
D. Drumlanrig Castle in Scotland

2. The thieves at Stockholm, Sweden, fled by this method.
A. Walking out
B. A Volkswagen Golf
C. A motorboat
D. A ladder

3. Thieves at the Isabella Stewart Gardner Museum disguised themselves as these.
A. Police officers
B. They didn't need to disguise themselves, as they were employees.
C. Tourists
D. Clergy

4. Leonardo da Vinci's *Madonna with the Yarnwinder* was recovered after a few months.
____ True
____ False

Answers on page 178.

WHAT CHANGED? PART I

Study this picture of the crime scene for 1 minute, then turn the page.

WHAT CHANGED? PART II

(Do not read this until you have read the previous page!)
From memory, can you tell what changed between this page and the previous page?

Answers on page 179.

SEEN AT THE SCENE PART I

Study this picture of the crime scene for 1 minute, then turn the page.

SEEN AT THE SCENE PART II

(Do not read this until you have read the previous page!)
Which image exactly matches the picture from the previous page?

1.

2.

3.

4.

Answers on page 179.

FIND THE WITNESS

There are 5 houses on Baker Avenue. You need to follow up with a witness, Laney Williams, but the paperwork only lists her street, not the specific address. You know from the previous interview that Williams is a single mother with full custody of her son. The staff at the corner coffee shop and your own observations give you some clues. From the information given, can you find the right house?

A. The widow in one corner house rents out her top floor to a college student.

B. The college student goes regularly to the other corner house to babysit the new baby of the couple who live there.

C. Williams mentioned to the staff at the coffee house that she donated some of her son's old toys to new baby. He was happy to give them away and wished the new baby was right next door!

D. Williams' son does like playing baseball with the kids his own age who live on either side of him.

House A House B House C House D House E

Answers on page 179.

INTERCEPTION

You've intercepted a message that is meant to reveal a location for an upcoming meeting between two criminal masterminds. The only problem is, the message shows many options. Can you figure out the right location?

EASTER ISLAND

STOCKHOLM SYNDROME

WART

SHROPSHIRE

INDIA

GTO

ONWARD

STADIUM

REVELATION

ETNA

DID YOU?

NEBRASKA

RASH

TSAR

EVER

ENTRANCE

AMORTIZE

Answers on page 179.

OVERHEARD INFORMATION PART I

Read the story below, then turn the page and answer the questions.

While on a train, a bystander overheard a man tell a woman about how best to rob a museum. The man said, "They do have a security guard monitoring the tapes, but he always takes his break from exactly midnight to 12:30, so you have a half-hour window. The other security guard will be making rounds during that time, but I'm going to leave a window open in the North side of the building. That's the first place he patrols, so with luck, he'll stay in that area fussing over the dollhouse exhibit. I plan to leave the window on the second floor of the gemstone exhibit on the East Wing unlocked. And remember, if you get caught and implicate me, I'm going to give evidence against you—and I have your fingerprints all over two paintings from 2004."

OVERHEARD INFORMATION PART II

(Do not read this until you have read the previous page!)

The bystander overheard the information about the crime that was planned, but didn't have anywhere to write it down! Answer the questions below to help the bystander remember what to tell the police.

1. The thieves mention two exhibits.
A. Masks and gems
B. Sculpture and gems
C. Gems and dollhouse
D. Dollhouse and carousel

2. One of the thieves was involved in an art theft in this year.
A. 2000
B. 2004
C. 2008
D. 2012

3. How many security guards will be on duty?
A. At least two
B. At least three
C. Four
D. Only one

4. The unlocked window will be found in this wing.
A. South
B. West
C. East
D. Basement

Answers on page 179.

SEEN AT THE SCENE PART 1

Study this picture of the crime scene for 1 minute, then turn the page.

SEEN AT THE SCENE PART II

(Do not read this until you have read the previous page!)
Which image exactly matches the picture from the previous page?

1.

2.

3.

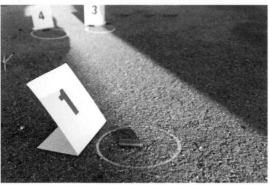

4.

Answers on page 179.

TREASURE HUNT

The investigator is tracking a jewelry thief's past trips in order to find and recover jewelry that was left behind in six cities. Each city was visited only once. Can you put together the travel timeline, using the information below?

1. The thief went to the city in the Southern hemisphere immediately before visiting the northernmost city on the list.

2. The visits to Reno and Miami were separated by either the trip to Philadelphia or the trip to Cabo San Lucas.

3. Lima was neither the first city visited nor the last.

4. The trip to Nevada was one of the first two stops.

5. The thief visited Vancouver sometime before visiting the city in Mexico.

Answers on page 179.

MOTEL HIDEOUT

A thief hides out in one of the 45 motel rooms listed in the chart below. The motel's in-house detective received a sheet of four clues, signed "The Logical Thief." Using these clues, the detective found the room number within 15 minutes—but by that time, the thief had fled. Can you find the thief's motel room more quickly?

1. **If you subtract the first digit from the second, the result is at least 1 but no larger than 4.**

2. **The number is not a multiple of 5 or 6.**

3. **If the digits were multiplied, the resulting number would be less than 20.**

4. **The number is the largest prime number that meets the first three conditions.**

51	52	53	54	55	56	57	58	59
41	42	43	44	45	46	47	48	49
31	32	33	34	35	36	37	38	39
21	22	23	24	25	26	27	28	29
11	12	13	14	15	16	17	18	19

Answers on page 179.

JAIL CELLS

Change just one letter on each line to go from the top word to the bottom word. Do not change the order of the letters. You must have a common English word at each step.

JAIL

———

———

CELL

FLEEING THE SCENE

Change just one letter on each line to go from the top word to the bottom word. Do not change the order of the letters. You must have a common English word at each step.

FLEES

———

———

shent (brought shame or discredit on)

———

SCENE

TRACK THE CRIMINAL

You are tracing the route of a criminal. You know he flew from Miami to Seattle, visiting each city once. You also know he chose the cheapest route for the trip. Can you trace the criminal's steps?

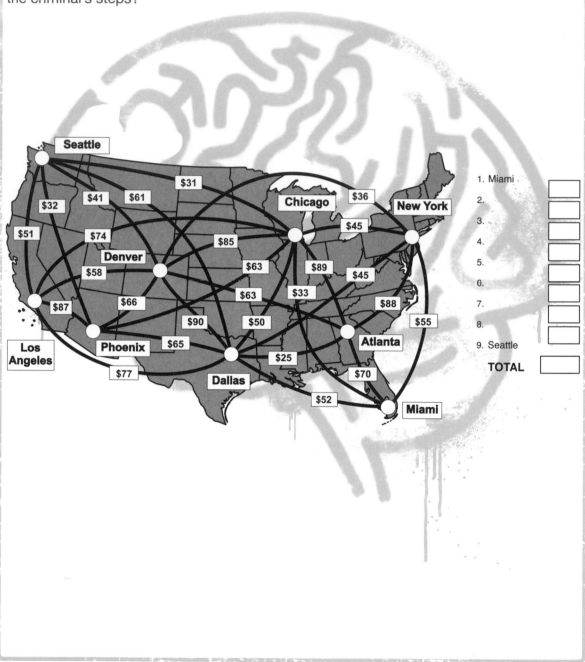

1. Miami
2.
3.
4.
5.
6.
7.
8.
9. Seattle

TOTAL

Answers on page 180.

WHAT WENT MISSING? PART I

The detective met his client on Monday, and was told that some old family documents were hidden somewhere in the room. This was the room in which they met. Examine the room, then turn the page.

WHAT WENT MISSING? PART II

(Do not read this until you have read the previous page!)

On Tuesday, the detective was called back because his client had disappeared. The detective noted that something else had gone missing. From memory, can you tell what changed between this page and the previous page?

Answers on page 180.

SEEN AT THE SCENE PART I

Study this picture of the crime scene for 1 minute, then turn the page.

SEEN AT THE SCENE PART II

(Do not read this until you have read the previous page!)
Which image exactly matches the picture from the previous page?

1.

2.

3.

4.

Answers on page 180.

OVERHEARD INFORMATION PART I

Read the story below, then turn the page and answer the questions.

While on a train, a bystander overheard a criminal tell an accomplice where a set of upcoming thefts would take place. The criminal said, "We're hitting up a bunch of stores on February 8, or February 10th if it snows on the 8th. But if it's raining, we're still on. This is the order: first the bakery on Lymon Street, then go to Marsh Street for the art gallery. Then we ditch the loot at the safehouse on Second Street before going across town to First Electronics on Fourth Street before going to ground."

OVERHEARD INFORMATION PART II

(Do not read this until you have read the previous page!)

The bystander overheard the information about the crimes that were planned, but didn't have anywhere to write it down! Answer the questions below to help the bystander remember what to tell the police.

1. The first location will be:
A. A bakery
B. An art gallery
C. A safehouse, to get supplies
D. An electronics store

2. The theft will take place on this day.
A. February 8
B. February 9
C. February 10
D. February 12

3. If it rains, the theft will take place on this day.
A. February 8
B. February 9
C. February 10
D. February 12

4. The electronics store is found on this street.
A. Lyman
B. Marsh
C. First
D. Fourth

64

Answers on page 180.

MOTEL HIDEOUT

A thief hides out in one of the 45 motel rooms listed in the chart below. The motel's in-house detective received a sheet of four clues, signed "The Logical Thief." Using these clues, the detective found the room number within 15 minutes—but by that time, the thief had fled. Can you find the thief's motel room more quickly?

1. If you multiply the digits together, the result will be a number on this chart.

2. The sum of the digits is greater than 9.

3. If you subtract the first digit from the second, the result is 5.

4. The number is not divisible by 19.

51	52	53	54	55	56	57	58	59
41	42	43	44	45	46	47	48	49
31	32	33	34	35	36	37	38	39
21	22	23	24	25	26	27	28	29
11	12	13	14	15	16	17	18	19

Answers on page 181.

TREASURE HUNT

The investigator is tracking a jewelry thief's past trips in order to find and recover jewelry that was left behind in six cities. Each city was visited only once. Can you put together the travel timeline, using the information below?

1. **Baltimore was one of the first three cities visited.**

2. **Detroit was one of the last three cities visited.**

3. **Toronto was visited either directly before or directly after Los Angeles.**

4. **The thief went directly from Seattle to Atlanta.**

5. **The trip did not begin or end on the Pacific coastline.**

6. **After visiting Baltimore, the thief visited three other cities before visiting Atlanta.**

Answers on page 181.

SEEN AT THE SCENE PART I

Study this picture of the crime scene for 1 minute, then turn the page.

SEEN AT THE SCENE PART II

(Do not read this until you have read the previous page!)
Which image exactly matches the picture from the previous page?

1.

2.

3.

4.

Answers on page 181.

FIND THE WITNESS

There are 5 houses on Lakeside Drive. You need to follow up with two witnesses, Marie and Carolyn West, but the paperwork only lists their street, not the specific address. You know from the previous interview that the couple does not have children. The staff at the corner coffee shop and your own observations give you some clues. From the information given, can you find the right house?

A. Four of the houses are home to couples, and the other owned by a widow.

B. The retired couple and the Wests come in together frequently, but are not next-door neighbors.

C. The newlyweds are next-door neighbors to the Wests.

D. The widow is glad she doesn't have to mow the lawn for a corner lot.

E. The couple who just sent their kid off to college wish he were still home, so he could mow their corner lot. The newlyweds joke that they'll have their own little lawn-mower to take care of their corner lot in a few years.

House A   House B   House C   House D   House E

Answers on page 181.

INTERCEPTION

You've intercepted a message. You think it might be the location of a meeting between two criminals, but it doesn't seem to make sense. Can you decipher the true message?

CELERY TOO TWO OAT AGAIN GAZING EARTHWARDS

FIXING RIVER ZOO VEER VANE

IS SOON NEW

NEAR OVAL BOO MOVE

WANE ILL RIG HAT PAT

Answers on page 181.

TREASURE HUNT

The investigator is tracking a jewelry thief's past trips in order to find and recover jewelry that was left behind in six cities. Each city was visited only once. Can you put together the travel timeline, using the information below?

1. The first and last locations were in the United States.

2. The thief went straight from Denver to Atlanta.

3. Seoul was one of the first three cities visited.

4. The thief went from Buenos Aires to a city in Europe.

5. Atlanta was one of the last three cities visited.

6. The thief did not go from Nashville to Athens, or vice versa.

Answers on page 181.

CRIME RHYMES

Each clue leads to a 2-word answer that rhymes, such as BIG PIG or STABLE TABLE. The numbers in parentheses after the clue give the number of letters in each word. For example, "cookware taken from the oven (3, 3)" would be "hot pot."

1. When the man who claimed to be a traveling preacher set a building on fire, it was known as the (6, 5): _____

2. The theft of several decorative containers was known as this (4, 4,): _____

3. When the criminal touched the dark piece of quartz, he left behind this (5, 5): _____

4. The burglar who stole from people while they were underwater exploring corals was known as this (4, 5): _____

5. An elaborate heist at the very tall building (10, 5): _____

6. When one shepherd killed another, it was known as this (6, 6): _____

7. To rob someone of a percussion instrument (5, 12): _____

8. The robbery of the elaborately-carved frozen sculptures was known as the (4, 5): _____

Answers on page 181.

WHAT WENT MISSING? PART I

The investigators were testing each other's attention to detail. Study this picture 1 minute, then turn the page.

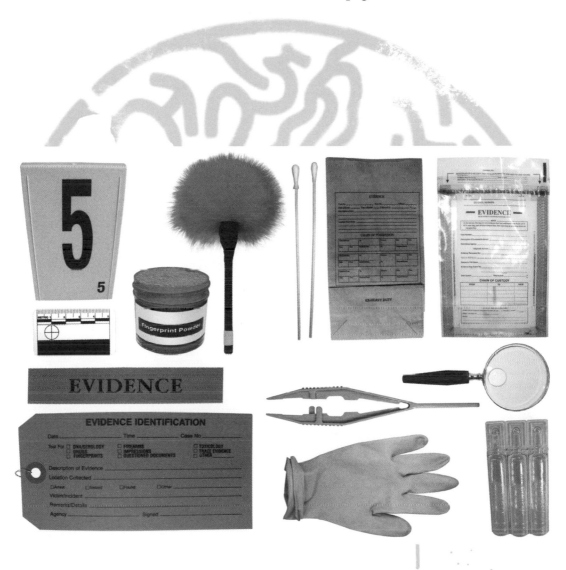

WHAT WENT MISSING? PART II

(Do not read this until you have read the previous page!)
The investigators removed one object from their colleague's workspace, and asked
what it was. From memory, can you work out which single object went missing?

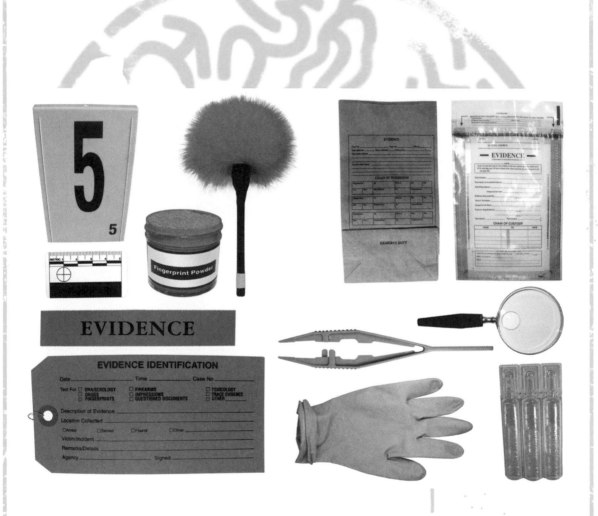

Answers on page 181.

OVERHEARD INFORMATION PART I

Read the story below, then turn the page and answer the questions.

While on a train, a bystander overheard a woman tell a thief about how best to rob an office. The woman said, "First, you got to promise not to steal any personal stuff from people, just the office stuff. Except from the CTO, you can take anything from his office, he's a jerk. They just got new computers for the Accounting department, really nice laptops, and those are along the East wall. The CEO has a safe in his office, behind the abstract painting, and the combination is 87-35-14.

OVERHEARD INFORMATION PART II

(Do not read this until you have read the previous page!)

The bystander overheard the information about the crimes that were planned, but didn't have anywhere to write it down! Answer the questions below to help the bystander remember what to tell the police.

1. The woman urges the man to steal from this person specifically.
A. The CFO
B. The CEO
C. The head accountant
D. The CTO

2. The newest laptops on the building are found along this wall.
A. North
B. South
C. East
D. West

3. The safe is found here.
A. In the CEO's office, underneath his desk
B. In the CEO's office, behind the abstract painting
C. In the CFO's office, behind the abstract painting
D. In the CTO's office, behind the Impressionist painting

4. This is the combination for the safe.
A. 87-35-14
B. 14-35-87
C. 35-14-87
D. 35-87-14

Answers on page 182.

THE COUNTERFEIT HOUSE PART I

Read this true crime account, then turn to the next page to test your knowledge.

On a hill overlooking the Ohio River in Monroe Township, Adams County, sits a house that isn't what it seems. Its modest size and quiet exterior hide countless architectural and historical secrets—secrets that have earned it the nickname "The Counterfeit House."

In 1850, Oliver Ezra Tompkins and his sister, Ann E. Lovejoy, purchased 118 acres and built a rather peculiar house to suit the needs of their successful home-based business. Tompkins and Lovejoy were counterfeiters who specialized in making fake 50-cent coins and $500 bills. They needed a house that could keep their secrets. Although passersby could see smoke escaping from the house's seven chimneys, only two of those chimneys were connected to working fireplaces; the others were fed by ductwork and filled with secret compartments. The front door featured a trick lock and a hidden slot for the exchange of money and products, and the gabled attic window housed a signal light.

The counterfeiting room was a windowless, doorless room in the rear of the house, accessible only through a series of trapdoors. A trapdoor in the floor led to a sizeable tunnel (big enough to fit a horse) that provided an escape route through the bedrock of the surrounding hills to a cliff.

While Lovejoy was in Cincinnati spending some of her counterfeit money, she was noticed by the police. A Pinkerton agent followed her home and watched as she opened the trick lock on the front door. He waited until she was inside, then followed her in.

Immediately past the door, in a 10-foot by 45-foot hallway, Tompkins was waiting—he beat the agent to death. Tompkins and Lovejoy buried the agent's body in one of the nearby hills, and Tompkins used the hidden tunnel to escape to a friendly riverboat, collapsing the tunnel with explosives as he went. Lovejoy held a mock funeral for Tompkins and inherited his estate, although shortly after she went into debt and moved away. There's a story that Lovejoy returned to the area the following year, with Tompkins's body—allegedly.

THE COUNTERFEIT HOUSE PART II

(Do not read this until you have read the previous page!)

1. Lovejoy and Tompkins specialized in forging these coins.
A. Penny
B. Quarter
C. 50-cent
D. Two-dollar

2. How many chimneys did the house have?
A. Two
B. Five
C. Seven
D. Nine

3. How many of those chimneys were connected to fireplaces?
A. Two
B. Five
C. Seven
D. Nine

4. A Pinkerton agent followed Tompkins back to the house.
____ True
____ False

Answers on page 182.

SEEN AT THE SCENE PART I

Study this picture of the crime scene for 1 minute, then turn the page.

SEEN AT THE SCENE PART II

(Do not read this until you have read the previous page!)
Which image exactly matches the picture from the previous page?

1.

2.

3.

4.

Answers on page 182.

MOTEL HIDEOUT

A thief hides out in one of the 45 motel rooms listed in the chart below. The motel's in-house detective received a sheet of four clues, signed "The Logical Thief." Using these clues, the detective found the room number within 15 minutes—but by that time, the thief had fled. Can you find the thief's motel room more quickly?

1. The number can be divided by 3.

2. The number is odd.

3. Neither of the digits is 5.

4. The first digit is larger than the second digit.

51	52	53	54	55	56	57	58	59
41	42	43	44	45	46	47	48	49
31	32	33	34	35	36	37	38	39
21	22	23	24	25	26	27	28	29
11	12	13	14	15	16	17	18	19

A MASTER FORGER PART I

Read this true crime account, then turn to page 84 to test your knowledge.

"Monet, Monet, Monet. Sometimes I get truly fed up doing Monet. Bloody haystacks." John Myatt's humorous lament sounds curiously Monty Pythonesque, until you realize that he can do Monet—and Chagall, Klee, Le Corbusier, Ben Nicholson, and almost any other painter you can name, great or obscure. Myatt, an artist of some ability, was probably the world's greatest art forger. He took part in an eight-year forgery scam in the 1980s and '90s that shook the foundations of the art world.

Despite what one might expect, art forgery is not a victimless crime. Many of Myatt's paintings—bought in good faith as the work of renowned masters—went for extremely high sums. One "Giacometti" sold at auction in New York for $300,000, and as many as 120 of his counterfeits are still out there, confusing and distressing the art world. But Myatt never set out to break the law.

Initially, Myatt would paint an unknown work in the style of one of the cubist, surrealist, or impressionist masters, and he seriously duplicated both style and subject. For a time, he gave them to friends or sold them as acknowledged fakes. Then he ran afoul of John Drewe.

Drewe was a London-based collector who had bought a dozen of Myatt's fakes over two years. Personable and charming, he ingratiated himself with Myatt by posing as a rich aristocrat. But one day he called and told Myatt that a cubist work the artist had done in the style of Albert Gleizes had just sold at Christies for £25,000 ($40,000)—as a genuine Gleizes. Drewe offered half of that money to Myatt.

The struggling artist was poor and taking care of his two children. The lure of the money was irresistible. So the scheme developed that he would paint a "newly discovered" work by a famous painter and pass it to Drewe, who would sell it and then pay Myatt his cut—usually about 10 percent. It would take Myatt two or three months to turn out a fake, and he was only making about £13,000 a year (roughly $21,000)—hardly worthy of a master criminal.

One of the amazing things about this scam was Myatt's materials. Most art forgers take great pains to duplicate the exact pigments used by the original artists, but Myatt mixed cheap emulsion house paint with a lubricating gel to get the colors he needed. One benefit is that his mix dried faster than oil paints.

But Drewe was just as much of a master forger, himself. The consummate con man, he inveigled his way into the art world through donations, talking his way into the archives of the Tate Gallery and learning every trick of provenance, the authentication of artwork. He faked letters from experts and, on one occasion, even inserted a phony catalog into the archives with pictures of Myatt's latest fakes as genuine.

But as the years went by, Myatt became increasingly worried about getting caught and going to prison, so at last he told Drewe he wanted out. Drewe refused to let him leave, and Myatt realized that his partner wasn't just in it for the money. He loved conning people.

The scam was not to last, of course. Drewe's ex-wife went to the police with incriminating documents, and when the trail led to Myatt's cottage in Staffordshire, he confessed.

Myatt served four months of a yearlong sentence, and when he came out of prison, Detective Superintendent Jonathan Searle of the Metropolitan Police was waiting for him. Searle suggested that since Myatt was now infamous, many people would love to own a real John Myatt fake. As a result, Myatt and his second wife Rosemary set up a tidy business out of their cottage. His paintings regularly sell for as much as £45,000 ($72,000), and Hollywood has shown interest in a movie—about the real John Myatt.

A MASTER FORGER PART II

(Do not read this until you have read the previous page!)

1. Who eventually went to the police and exposed the con?
A. Myatt
B. Myatt's ex-wife
C. Drewe
D. Drewe's ex-life

2. Before Drewe brought Myatt into the scheme, he bought some "acknowledged fakes" but sold them as genuine.
____ True
____ False

3. Myatt took about this percent of the proceeds.
A. 10%
B. 25%
C. 50%
D. 90%

4. Myatt served four years in prison.
____ True
____ False

84

Answers on page 182.

FIRST STEAL, THEN FLEE

Change just one letter on each line to go from the top word to the bottom word. Do not change the order of the letters. You must have a common English word at each step.

STEAL

_____

_____

_____

_____

FLEES

WILL A PLOT LEAD TO JAIL?

Change just one letter on each line to go from the top word to the bottom word. Do not change the order of the letters. You must have a common English word at each step.

PLOT

_____

_____

_____

_____

JAIL

FINGERPRINT MATCH

Find the matching fingerprint(s). There may be more than one.

A.

B.

C.

D.

E.

F.

G.

H.

I.

J.

K.

L.

86

Answers on page 182.

SEEN AT THE SCENE PART I

Study this picture of the crime scene for 1 minute, then turn the page.

SEEN AT THE SCENE PART II

(Do not read this until you have read the previous page!)
Which image exactly matches the picture from the previous page?

1.

2.

3.

4.

Answers on page 182.

FIND THE WITNESS

On Plum Street, there are 5 houses. You need to follow up with a witness, Melanie Shah, but the paperwork only lists her street, not the specific address. You know that Shah is a divorced woman who lives by herself. The staff at the coffee shop around the corner and your own observations give you some clues. From the information given, can you find the right house?

A. One member of the wait staff says Shah recently mentioned repainting her house blue. There are two blue houses on the street.

B. Another member of the wait staff knows that a family lives in house D.

C. House B is yellow.

D. House C is green.

E. House E is white.

House A   House B   House C   House D   House E

TREASURE HUNT

The investigator is tracking a jewelry thief's past trips in order to find and recover jewelry that was left behind in six cities. Each city was visited only once. Can you put together the travel timeline, using the information below?

1. The jewel thief's last stop was in the United States.

2. The thief visited Panama City, Phoenix, and Portland in a row, but not necessarily in that order.

3. The thief went directly from Mexico to Canada, without stopping in the U.S. along the way.

4. Memphis was one of the first two cities visited.

5. The visits to Acapulco and Panama City were separated by one other city.

6. The visits between Edmonton and a city in the Pacific Northwest were separated by one other city.

Answers on page 183.

INTERCEPTION

You've intercepted a message that is meant to reveal a location for an upcoming meeting between two criminal masterminds. The only problem is, the message shows many place names. Can you figure out the right location?

RABAT

GHENT

YAREN

MALTA

QUITO

TUNIS

Answers on page 183.

MOTEL HIDEOUT

A thief hides out in one of the 45 motel rooms listed in the chart below. The motel's in-house detective received a sheet of four clues, signed "The Logical Thief." Using these clues, the detective found the room number within 15 minutes—but by that time, the thief had fled. Can you find the thief's motel room more quickly?

1. The sum of the digits is less than 10.

2. The sum of the digits is greater than 5.

3. The first digit is larger than the second digit.

4. The second digit is divisible by 4.

51	52	53	54	55	56	57	58	59
41	42	43	44	45	46	47	48	49
31	32	33	34	35	36	37	38	39
21	22	23	24	25	26	27	28	29
11	12	13	14	15	16	17	18	19

Answers on page 183.

OVERHEARD INFORMATION PART I

Read the story below, then turn the page and answer the questions.

While on a train, a bystander overheard one man tell another about how best to rob an office. The man said, "Okay, this is the keycard. It's deactivated so it'll show as a temp employee as logging in. Petty cash is in the cube of the CFO's assistant, across from his office, Billy Thompson. She's Renee Thompson, no relation. I think she keeps the cash in the second cabinet drawer. Most of the art is just prints, but there are some good pieces in the CEO's conference room. The extra company laptops that they give out for travel are in the office of the head of IT. She's got a separate code to her office, and I think it's 21-45-93. But if it doesn't work, you can only try again once, because a third wrong try will set off an alarm. And I don't care how much you manage to get or don't get, I get my payment regardless."

OVERHEARD INFORMATION PART II

(Do not read this until you have read the previous page!)

The bystander overheard the information about the crime that was planned, but didn't have anywhere to write it down! Answer the questions below to help the bystander remember what to tell the police.

1. The keycard will show this employee logging in.
A. Billy Thompson
B. Renee Thompson
C. The head of IT
D. None of the above

2. Which two employees have the same name but no relation?
A. The CEO and his assistant
B. The CFO and his assistant
C. The CFO and the head of IT
D. The CEO and the head of IT

3. The code to access the room where spare laptops are kept is:
A. 45-21-93
B. 93-21-45
C. 21-45-93
D. 22-45-93

4. The man is giving information to the thief because he expects to receive this.
A. An unspecified payment
B. A percentage of the haul
C. A particular piece of art from the CEO's office
D. He doesn't want a monetary reward, just revenge

Answers on page 183.

WHAT CHANGED? PART I

Study this picture of the crime scene for 1 minute, then turn the page.

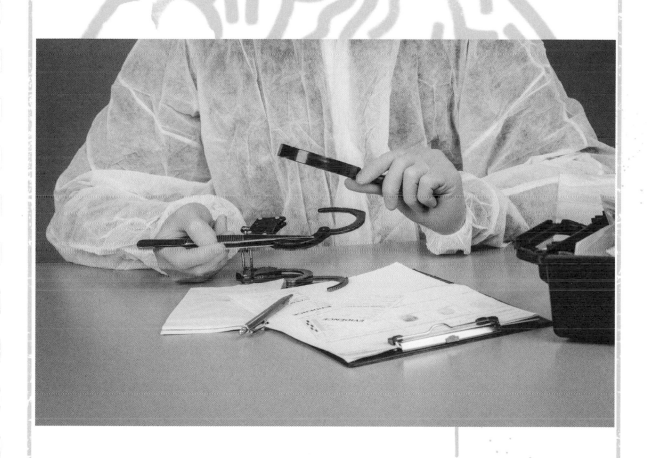

WHAT CHANGED? PART II

(Do not read this until you have read the previous page!)
From memory, can you tell what changed between this page and the previous page?

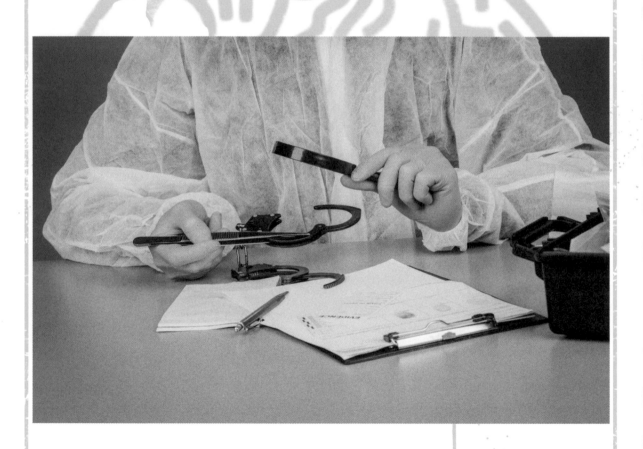

Answers on page 183.

SEEN AT THE SCENE PART I

Study this picture of the crime scene for 1 minute, then turn the page.

SEEN AT THE SCENE PART II

(Do not read this until you have read the previous page!)
Which image exactly matches the picture from the previous page?

1.

2.

3.

4.

Answers on page 183.

NOTHING TO DO WITH DOYLE

Cryptograms are messages in substitution code. Break the code to read the message. For example, THE SMART CAT might become FVO QWGDF JGF if **F** is substituted for **T,** **V** for **H, O** for **E,** and so on.

C.C. CLHIBR VGRK'S G JDYSDLKGH NBSBYSDUB—
CB VGR G RBQDGH FDHHBQ, LJSBK YLKRDNBQBN
SCB JDQRS DK GIBQDYG. PLQK CBQIGK VBPRSBQ
ITNABSS DK 1861, CB YLKJBRRBN SL 27 ITQNBQR PTS
IGX CGUB PBBK QBRMLKRDPHB JLQ ILQB. CB VGR
GHRL G PDAGIDRS, IGQQDBN SL SCQBB VLIBK GS
SCB SDIB LJ CDR NBGSC.

VALACHI SPEAKS PART I

Read this true crime account, then turn to page 102 to test your knowledge.

On June 22, 1962, in the federal penitentiary in Atlanta, Georgia, a man serving a sentence of 15 to 20 years for heroin trafficking picked up a steel pipe and murdered another convict. The killer was Joseph "Joe Cargo" Valachi; the intended victim was Joseph DiPalermo—but Valachi got the wrong man and killed another inmate, Joe Saupp. This mistake touched off one of the greatest criminal revelations in history.

Joe Valachi, a 59-year-old Mafia "soldier," was the first member of the Mafia to publicly acknowledge the reality of that criminal organization—making La Cosa Nostra (which means "this thing of ours") a household name. He opened the doors to expose an all-pervasive, wide-ranging conglomerate of crime families, the existence of which was repeatedly denied by J. Edgar Hoover and the FBI. By testifying against his own organization, Valachi violated omerta, the code of silence.

Vito Genovese was the boss of New York's powerful Genovese crime family. Valachi had worked for the family for much of his life—primarily as a driver, but also as a hit man, enforcer, numbers runner, and drug pusher. When Valachi was on his way to prison after having been found guilty of some of these activities, Genovese believed the small-time operator had betrayed him to obtain a lighter sentence for himself. So Genovese put a $100,000 bounty on Valachi's head. He and Valachi were actually serving sentences in the same prison when Valachi killed Joe Saupp—mistaking him for Joseph DiPalermo, whom he thought had been assigned by Genovese to murder him. Whether or not Valachi had broken the code of silence and betrayed Genovese before the bounty was placed on his head, he certainly did it with a vengeance afterward.

But why did Valachi turn informer? The answer to that question isn't entirely clear. Most speculate that Valachi was afraid of a death sentence for killing Saupp and agreed to talk to the Feds in exchange for a lighter sentence.

Valachi was a barely literate, street-level miscreant whose knowledge of the workings of the organization was limited. However, when he was brought before John L. McClellan's Senate Permanent Investigations Subcommittee in October 1963, he began talking beyond his personal experience, relaying urban legends as truth, and painting a picture of the Mafia that was both fascinating and chilling.

All in all, Joe Valachi helped identify 317 members of the Mafia. His assistance gave Attorney General Robert Kennedy "a significant addition to the broad picture of organized crime." Unlike Hoover, Bobby Kennedy had no problem acknowledging the Mafia. (One theory about Hoover's denials is that they were a result of long-term Mafia blackmail regarding his homosexuality.)

Valachi's revelations ran the gamut from minor accuracies to babbling exaggerations, as well as from true to false, but the cat was out of the bag. Americans became fascinated with crime families, codes of honor, gang wars, hit killings, and how widely the Mafia calamari had stretched its tentacles. Very private criminals suddenly found their names splashed across headlines and blaring from televisions. During the next three years in the New York–New Jersey–Connecticut metropolitan area, more organized criminals were arrested and jailed than in the previous 30 years. Whatever safe conduct pass the Mafia may have held had expired.

When journalist Peter Maas interviewed Valachi and came out with *The Valachi Papers*, the U.S. Department of Justice first encouraged but then tried to block its publication. Regardless, the book was released in 1968. This work soon became the basis of a movie that starred Charles Bronson as Joe Valachi. The novel *The Godfather* was published in 1969, and in the film *The Godfather: Part II*, the characters of Willie Cicci and Frank Pentangeli were reportedly inspired by Valachi.

The $100,000 bounty on the life of Joseph Valachi was never claimed. In 1966, Valachi unsuccessfully attempted to hang himself in his prison cell using an electrical cord. Five years later, he died of a heart attack at La Tuna Federal Correctional Institution in Texas. He had outlived his chief nemesis, Genovese, by two years.

VALACHI SPEAKS PART II

(Do not read this until you have read the previous page!)

1. This means a code of silence.
A. Casa Nostra
B. Mafia
C. Omerta
D. Genovese

2. This was the size of the bounty on Valachi's head.
A. $10,000
B. $50,000
C. $100,000
D. 1 million dollars

3. Valachi testified to this committee.
A. Senate Permanent Investigations Subcommittee
B. Senate Organized Crime Committee
C. House Investigations Committee
D. House Investigations and Informants Subcommittee

4. The Valachi Papers was released in this year.
A. 1962
B. 1963
C. 1968
D. 1969

Answers on page 184.

OVERHEARD INFORMATION PART I

Read the story below, then turn the page and answer the questions.

While on a train, a bystander overheard a criminal tell an accomplice where a set of upcoming thefts would take place. The thief said, "On June 8th we hit the jewelry store at Rivers Edgetown Mall, the one on the first floor, not the one near the anchor store. On June 10th we've got someone on the inside who will turn off the surveillance video at the electronics place on the strip mall on 7th and Main. Then we lie low for a week before hitting the shoe store on Butterlake Drive on June 19th."

OVERHEARD INFORMATION PART II

Do not read this until you have read the previous page!)

The bystander overheard the information about the crimes that were planned, but didn't have anywhere to write it down! Answer the questions below to help the bystander remember what to tell the police.

1. The jewelry store is found here.
A. The first floor at Rivers Edgetown Mall
B. Near the anchor store at Rivers Edgetown Mall
C. The strip mall on Edgetown and Main
D. The strip mall on 7th and Main

2. The thieves have an accomplice at this location.
A. Jewelry store
B. Shoe store
C. Bicycle store
D. Electronics store

3. The shoe store is found on this street.
A. Butterlake Avenue
B. Butterlake Lane
C. Butterlake Drive
D. Butterlake Court

4. The theft at the electronics place is scheduled for this day.
A. June 8
B. June 10
C. June 18
D. June 19

Answers on page 184.

SEEN AT THE SCENE PART I

Study this picture of the crime scene for 1 minute, then turn the page.

SEEN AT THE SCENE PART II

(Do not read this until you have read the previous page!)
Which image exactly matches the picture from the previous page?

1.

2.

3.

4.

Answers on page 184.

FIND THE WITNESS

On Riggins Street, there are 5 houses. You need to follow up with a witness, Catalina Ramirez, but the paperwork only lists her street, not the specific address. You know that Ramirez lives with her teenaged son and a boyfriend. The staff at the coffee shop around the corner and your own observations give you some clues. From the information given, can you find the right house?

A. The people who live in the house A always help the elderly couple next door, whose children live far away, shovel their walkway.

B. The elderly couple also get help from another retired couple, who drive them to the grocery store each week.

C. The couple in house D just put out a stork figurine to celebrate their new baby.

D. One of the corner houses is vacant while it's being sold.

House A   House B   House C   House D   House E

INTERCEPTION

You've intercepted a message that is meant to reveal a location for an upcoming meeting between two criminal masterminds. The only problem is, the message shows many place names. Can you figure out the right location?

BANGKOK

ATLANTA

BOSTON

ARKANSAS

OTTAWA

HONDURAS

DOMINICAN REPUBLIC

TRIPOLI

RABAT

PARAGUAY

Answers on page 184.

TREASURE HUNT

The investigator is tracking a jewelry thief's past trips in order to find and recover jewelry that was left behind in six cities. Each city was visited only once. Can you put together the travel timeline, using the information below?

1. **Chicago was one of the first four cities visited.**

2. **One of the Canadian cities was the first visited, and the other was the last.**

3. **The thief flew directly from San Diego to Rio de Janeiro.**

4. **The thief flew directly from Chicago to Boston, or vice versa.**

5. **The thief did not fly from Rio to either Calgary or Vancouver.**

6. **The two cities on the Pacific coastline were visited one after the other.**

MOTEL HIDEOUT

A thief hides out in one of the 45 motel rooms listed in the chart below. The motel's in-house detective received a sheet of four clues, signed "The Logical Thief." Using these clues, the detective found the room number within 15 minutes—but by that time, the thief had fled. Can you find the thief's motel room more quickly?

1. The number is even.

2. The sum of the digits is odd.

3. Either the number 4 is one of the digits or the number is divisible by 4, but not both.

4. The sum of the digits is greater than 10.

51	52	53	54	55	56	57	58	59
41	42	43	44	45	46	47	48	49
31	32	33	34	35	36	37	38	39
21	22	23	24	25	26	27	28	29
11	12	13	14	15	16	17	18	19

Answers on page 184.

OVERHEARD INFORMATION PART I

Read the story below, then turn the page and answer the questions.

An investigator hears a conversation between two criminals, in which one tells the other the passwords to the underground gambling clubs run through his chain of restaurants. He hears, "At the River Square location, ask for Matty and tell him, 'Ducks are the most beautiful birds.' At North Peak Plaza, ask for Patrick and tell him, 'I've met your cousin Louise, isn't she the best?' But Patrick's only there Monday, Wednesday, and Friday. Don't go to the strip mall on Waverly Place until things cool down, since we almost had a bust there. Unless you want their dumplings, because they do have the best dumplings there."

OVERHEARD INFORMATION PART II

(Do not read this until you have read the previous page!)

1. Who is in charge at the River Square location?

_____

2. What is the password at the North Peak Plaza location?

_____

3. What days is the North Peak Plaza location active?

_____

4. What is the name of the location with the dumplings?

_____

Answers on page 184.

SEEN AT THE SCENE PART I

Study this picture of the crime scene for 1 minute, then turn the page.

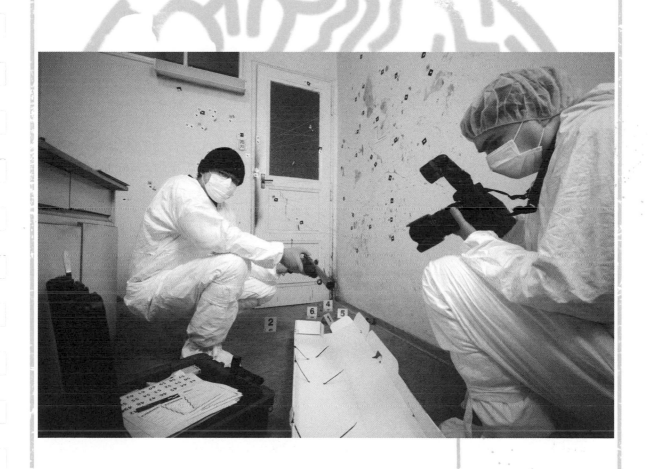

SEEN AT THE SCENE PART II

(Do not read this until you have read the previous page!)
Which image exactly matches the picture from the previous page?

1.

2.

3.

4.

Answers on page 184.

LEAVING CLUES

Change just one letter on each line to go from the top word to the bottom word. Do not change the order of the letters. You must have a common English word at each step.

LEAVE

_____

_____

_____

_____ **synonym for burns**

_____

_____

_____

_____

CLUES

CRIME SCENE

ACROSS

1. No place for a roller skate
6. Football or badminton
11. One-named author of "A Dog of Flanders"
12. Jouster's protection
13. It's collected at a crime scene
15. Countess's counterpart
16. Ending with Siam or Japan
17. "But of course!"
20. "Naked Maja" painter
22. Sheriffs and marshals, e.g.
24. After-dinner treat
28. "Precious bodily fluid" that may be found at a crime scene
29. Telltale strand that may be found at a crime scene
30. Realtor sign add-on
31. Slangy physician
32. "Good gravy!"
34. It's above the horizon
35. Belonging to the Thing?
38. Metals in the raw
40. They provide a permanent record of a crime scene
45. Font feature
46. Fields of expertise
47. Jets, to Sharks
48. Garment size

DOWN

1. Fastest way to a new lawn
2. Large cask for wine
3. Org. for Saarinen
4. Concept for Colette
5. Devastated
6. "I'm sorry to say..."
7. Canada's Grand ___ National Historic Park
8. Everything: Lat.
9. Fabled giant birds
10. Sequoia or sycamore
14. Fe, to a chemist
17. Church robes
18. Metaphor for purity
19. Derelict GI
21. Between
23. Pop music's Depeche___
25. Bird of the Nile
26. Giraffe's trademark
27. Homer's besieged city
29. FBI part
31. "CSI" star Helgenberger
33. He was originally called Dippy Dawg
35. ___ dixit (unproven assertion)
36. Back in those days
37. Aching
39. "Love Song" singer Bareilles
41. Bob Cratchit's son
42. Miles ___ hour
43. Crone
44. Direction opposite NNW

FINGERPRINT MATCH

Find the matching fingerprint(s). There may be more than one.

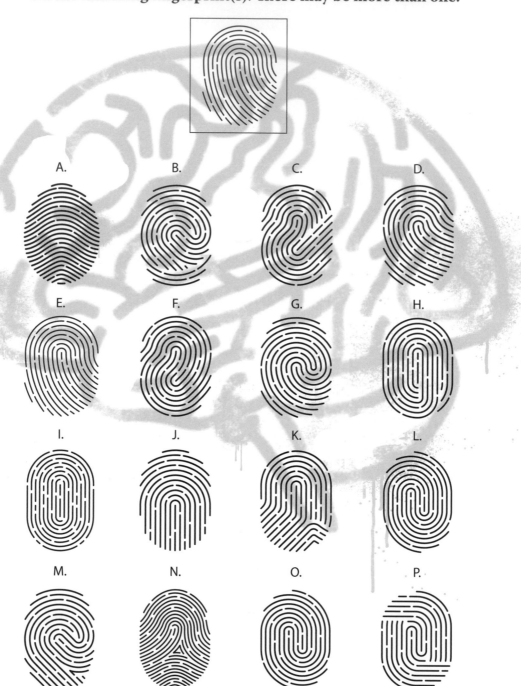

A.

B.

C.

D.

E.

F.

G.

H.

I.

J.

K.

L.

M.

N.

O.

P.

Answers on page 185.

CRACK THE PASSWORD

The thief left behind a list of scrambled passwords. This puzzle functions exactly like an anagram with an added step: In addition to being scrambled, each word below is missing the same letter. Discover the missing letter, then unscramble the words to reveal the list of passwords.

MORBID

COINED

RETRAIN

VELATE

CRACK THE PASSWORD

The thief left behind a list of scrambled passwords. This puzzle functions exactly like an anagram with an added step: In addition to being scrambled, each word below is missing the same letter. Discover the missing letter, then unscramble the words to reveal the list of passwords.

MINCED

RAGBAG

GOOGLY

GAUCHO

MOTEL HIDEOUT

A thief hides out in one of the 45 motel rooms listed in the chart below. The motel's in-house detective received a sheet of four clues, signed "The Logical Thief." Using these clues, the detective found the room number within 15 minutes—but by that time, the thief had fled. Can you find the thief's motel room more quickly?

1. **The second digit is a multiple of 3.**

2. **The number is prime.**

3. **The sum of the digits is greater than 10.**

4. **The first digit is more than half the second digit.**

51	52	53	54	55	56	57	58	59
41	42	43	44	45	46	47	48	49
31	32	33	34	35	36	37	38	39
21	22	23	24	25	26	27	28	29
11	12	13	14	15	16	17	18	19

120

Answers on page 186.

WHAT CHANGED? PART I

Study this picture of the crime scene for 1 minute, then turn the page.

WHAT CHANGED? PART II

(Do not read this until you have read the previous page!)
From memory, can you tell what changed between this page and the previous page?

Answers on page 186.

FIND THE WITNESS

There are 5 houses on Jenkins Street. You need to follow up with a witness, Tom Beal, but the paperwork only lists the street, not the specific address. You know that Beal lives by himself but that he was out walking his dog a few blocks away when he saw the crime. The staff at the bakery around the corner and your own observations give you some clues. From the information given, can you find the right house?

A. One staff member says she has definitely heard barking from both houses B and E when she walks past them to get to the bus stop. She's not sure about the other houses.

B. The shop's manager says that a retired couple lives in house D. They often babysit for the two families on the street who have younger children.

C. Another staff member knows the child in house A has allergies that prevent his parents from getting any pets.

D. The two teenagers in the middle house often have pool parties. One teenager has taught the younger children who lives next door to swim.

House A   House B   House C   House D   House E

Answers on page 186.

INTERCEPTION

You've intercepted a message that is meant to reveal a location for an upcoming meeting between two criminal masterminds. The only problem is, the message shows many place names. Can you figure out the right location?

MINSK

CAIRO

DELHI

KABUL

ABUJA

VADUZ

Answers on page 186.

TREASURE HUNT

The investigator is tracking a jewelry thief's past trips in order to find and recover jewelry that was left behind in six cities. Each city was visited only once. Can you put together the travel timeline, using the information below?

1. From Minneapolis the thief immediately flew further north.

2. Washington, D.C., was one of the final two cities.

3. Winnipeg was visited sometime before Orlando.

4. From Guadalajara the thief went directly to Seattle.

5. The first city was in the United States.

6. At least one city was visited between the city in Florida and the nation's capital.

CRIME RHYMES

Each clue leads to a 2-word answer that rhymes, such as BIG PIG or STABLE TABLE. The numbers in parentheses after the clue give the number of letters in each word. For example, "cookware taken from the oven (3, 3)" would be "hot pot."

1. A smooth, carefully-executed robbery might be called this (4, 5): _____

2. The suspect had a witness that he was baking desserts at the time of the crime, giving him this (3, 5): _____

3. The arsonist was said to do this (6, 4): _____

4. To pick up someone who might have done the crime for questioning (7, 7): _____

5. This resentful forger of money gave information on his former colleagues (6, 13): _____

6. The private detective who had a side job as a toll collector was called this (9, 6): _____

7. The robbery in the nautical museum was called this (8, 5): _____

8. The plan to defraud the lottery was known as this (7, 4): _____

Answers on page 186.

OVERHEARD INFORMATION PART I

Read the story below, then turn the page and answer the questions.

While on a train, a bystander overheard a conversation where one person was giving another the passwords for a set of underground gambling clubs. The bystander heard that the password for the downtown club was, "Do you have the zucchini lasagna on the menu tonight?" At the near north location, the password was, "You have the most delicious brownies for dessert, pass my compliments to the chef!" At the east side location, the password is, "Is Lon in the kitchen tonight? He makes the best burgers." At the west side location, the password is, "Do you know if the salad dressing has MSG?"

OVERHEARD INFORMATION PART II

(Do not read this until you have read the previous page!)

As the undercover investigator charged with going into the clubs, you'll need to know the passwords. How many do you remember?

West side: _____

Downtown: _____

Near north: _____

East side: _____

Answers on page 186.

SEEN AT THE SCENE PART I

Study this picture of the crime scene for 1 minute, then turn the page.

SEEN AT THE SCENE PART II

(Do not read this until you have read the previous page!)

1. What weapon is found near evidence marker 1?
_____ Knife
_____ Gun

2. The investigator's suitcase is:
_____ Open
_____ Closed

3. An evidence marker is found directly to the investigator's left.
_____ True
_____ False

4. The investigator is wearing a face mask.
_____ True
_____ False

Answers on page 186.

TEST THE ALIBI

Detectives are investigating a murder. The victim, Christina Jones, had a video call with a friend that ended at 8 PM. Her roommate discovered the body when she returned home at midnight. The prime suspect, Brian Smith, has an alibi. He was seen a twenty-minute drive away at a large party with numerous guests between 7 PM and 2 AM. The detectives are trying to see if there is a time window of one hour when he could have left the party and committed the murder. While many people attest to seeing Brian at the party, only these witness statements list a specific time. From them, can you verify the alibi?

Statement from J.A., the host: "Oh, he was definitely here. He was one of the first ones to arrive—I'd said 7, but he and Karen showed up around a quarter after. He and Karen helped me set up the snacks before other people starting arriving. Then a bunch of other people started arriving probably around 7:30 or so and I went out to meet them. I saw him a couple times after that, I'm not sure of times, but I didn't get a chance to talk to him. He drifted out probably around 1:30."

Statement from W.R., who had not met Brian before that night but recognized his picture: "We had a conversation about Game of Thrones earlier in the evening— sometime between 9 and 10, but I'm not sure exactly. I left at 10, though, so it was before that. Probably closer to 9."

Statement from T.R., a friend of Brian's: "No, no, he was absolutely at the party. We took a selfie, see?" (The timestamp on the selfie registered at 8:25 PM.) "And then we talked for a while after that, and I saw him in a card game with Tina and that crowd later on. I'm not sure what time, maybe 10? 11?"

Statement from Tina: "I didn't get there until 9, and we didn't start playing right away. But yes, he was in a card game with us. Maybe 9:30 to 10:30? It wasn't a long card game. I think I saw him later but I'm not sure when."

The bartender hired for the party has credit card receipts for drinks at 7:45 PM, 9:30 PM, and 12:30 AM.

MAFIA BUSTER PART I

Read the story below, than turn to page 134 and answer the questions.

The name Joseph Petrosino means nothing to most New Yorkers—unless they're police officers, who regard the guy as a legend. In the first decade of the 20th century, Petrosino established himself as one of the toughest, most effective detectives in NYPD history. His beat was Little Italy, and he spent much of his career going toe-to-toe with the Mafia. It was a war that ultimately cost him his life.

Petrosino was brought into the department by Captain Alexander Williams, who had watched Petrosino tangle with local thugs on the city streets. Petrosino didn't meet the police height requirement, but in addition to being tough as nails, he spoke fluent Italian and was familiar with the local culture. Williams quickly realized that Petrosino could be an invaluable asset to the force.

The NYPD put Petrosino to work as a sergeant in 1883. He wasted no time making his presence known within the city's Italian community. Strong and fearless, Petrosino became a brawler when necessary, but he also knew the value of quiet detective work. (Dedication and fearlessness eventually elevated him to the rank of lieutenant.) To gather intelligence, for instance, Petrosino routinely disguised himself as a tunnel "sandhog" laborer, a blind street beggar, and other urban denizens who can slip around unnoticed.

Petrosino solved plenty of crimes during his career, but it was his labor to eliminate the vicious gangs preying on Italian immigrants that made him famous. Italian gangsters started setting up shop in the city around 1900, bringing murder, theft, and extortion with them. Petrosino made it his mission to end their reign of terror.

Foremost among Petrosino's gangland foes was Vito Cascio Ferro, whom some consider one of the inspirations for Mario Puzo's The Godfather. Ferro arrived in New York from Sicily in 1901, already a mob boss to be feared and respected. Petrosino made no secret of his desire to implicate Ferro in the gruesome murder in which a body had been dismembered and stuffed in a barrel. As Petrosino closed in, Ferro fled to Sicily, vowing revenge.

Meanwhile, Petrosino continued to battle the various gangs plaguing Little Italy. Kidnapping and murder were on the rise, as was the use of bombs. (In one terrifying incident, Petrosino managed to extinguish a bomb's fuse with his fingers just seconds before the bomb was set to explode.) Determined to stay ahead of the criminals, Petrosino established the nation's first bomb squad, teaching himself and his crew how to dismantle the deadly devices.

In 1908, Vito Ferro again attempted to reach into New York, this time through an intermediary—a murderous Sicilian named Raffaele Palizzolo. At first, clueless city officials embraced Palizzolo, who claimed to want to eliminate the Black Hand, as the Mafia was also called. But Petrosino was skeptical and tailed Palizzolo everywhere. This forced Palizzolo to return to Sicily, much to Ferro's anger.

Petrosino's boss, Police Commissioner Theodore Bingham, was eager to eliminate New York's Mafia menace once and for all. Early in 1909 he sent Petrosino on a clandestine trip to Italy to meet with law enforcement officials there and gather intelligence. Because the underworld had put a price on his head, Petrosino made the trip disguised as a Jewish merchant named Simone Velletri. Unfortunately, his mission didn't remain a secret for long: While Petrosino was still in transit, the *New York Herald* ran a story that he was on his way to Italy specifically to gather information on Italian gangsters. The source? Bingham, who had stupidly confided in a reporter.

By the time Petrosino arrived in Italy, news of his mission had spread throughout the local underworld. Ferro ordered a hit. On March 12, 1909, two gunmen cut down Petrosino.

The detective's funeral was one of the largest in New York history. Thousands of police officers and citizens lined the streets as the procession traveled through the city to Calvary Cemetery in Long Island.

MAFIA BUSTER PART II

(Do not read this until you have read the previous page!)

1. Petrosino's mentor, this man brought him onto the force.

_____

2. What was the name of Petrosino's main foe?

_____

3. This man leaked the information that got Petrosino killed.

_____

4. Name three disguises Petrosino used at various points.

_____

_____

_____

Answers on page 187.

MOTEL HIDEOUT

A thief hides out in one of the 45 motel rooms listed in the chart below. The motel's in-house detective received a sheet of four clues, signed "The Logical Thief." Using these clues, the detective found the room number within 15 minutes—but by that time, the thief had fled. Can you find the thief's motel room more quickly?

1. The number is odd.

2. The sum of the digits is even.

3. The number is not prime.

4. Add 4 to the first digit to get the second digit.

51	52	53	54	55	56	57	58	59
41	42	43	44	45	46	47	48	49
31	32	33	34	35	36	37	38	39
21	22	23	24	25	26	27	28	29
11	12	13	14	15	16	17	18	19

A LONG PATH FROM CRIME TO TRIAL

Change just one letter on each line to go from the top word to the bottom word. Do not change the order of the letters. You must have a common English word at each step.

CRIME

_____

_____

_____

_____

_____

_____ **sets of two**

_____

_____

_____

_____

_____

_____

TRIAL

Answers on page 187.

OVERHEARD INFORMATION PART I

Read the story below, then turn the page and answer the questions.

While on a train, a bystander overheard a conversation between two men talking about how best to rob a restaurant.

The first man says, "They lock up their money in the safe each night, and Kerri's given me the combo. 05-36-29. They don't take it to the bank until Friday, so I think we go Thursday night after they close."

The second man says, "I've scoped out the video situation. They don't use their cameras to record—they just have them there to deter robberies. But the store on the left, the antique shop, does keep cameras running—so we have to approach and leave from the corner on the left."

OVERHEARD INFORMATION PART II

(Do not read this until you have read the previous page!)

1. The bystander hears a conversation between these two people.
A. Two men
B. A man and a woman
C. Two teenagers
D. Two women

2. The combo for the safe is:
A. 36-29-05
B. 29-36-05
C. 05-29-36
D. 05-36-29

3. The theft is planned for this night.
A. Wednesday
B. Thursday
C. Friday
D. Saturday

4. The name of the accomplice inside the restaurant who gave the safe code is:
A. Kitty
B. Kerri
C. Kelli
D. Karen

Answers on page 187.

WHAT CHANGED? PART I

Study this picture of the crime scene for 1 minute, then turn the page.

WHAT CHANGED? PART II

(Do not read this until you have read the previous page!)
From memory, can you tell what changed between this page and the previous page?

Answers on page 187.

SEEN AT THE SCENE PART I

Study this picture of the crime scene for 1 minute, then turn the page.

SEEN AT THE SCENE PART II

(Do not read this until you have read the previous page!)
Which image exactly matches the picture from the previous page?

1.

2.

3.

4.

Answers on page 187.

FIND THE WITNESS

There are five houses on Jarvis Lane. You need to gather a witness statement from Michel and Tanya Stoven, but without any address on the doors you are not sure which house to approach. You know that the Stovens have two teenaged daughters. The staff at the coffee shop around the corner and your own observations give you some clues. From the information given, can you find the right house?

A. There are kids at four of the houses.

B. The single dad lives next to the bachelor who is in one corner house.

C. The single mom likes the big lot she has at the other corner house.

D. Stoven's younger daughter babysits for the single dad next door.

House A   House B   House C   House D   House E

Answers on page 187.

INTERCEPTION

You've intercepted a message that is meant to reveal a location for an upcoming meeting between two criminal masterminds. The only problem is, the message shows many place names. Can you figure out the right location?

ABU DHABI

BARBADOS

ARGENTINA

ICELAND

BEIJING

ALBANIA

SOFIA

ANDORRA

GAMBIA

Answers on page 188.

FINGERPRINT MATCH

Find the matching fingerprint(s). There may be more than one.

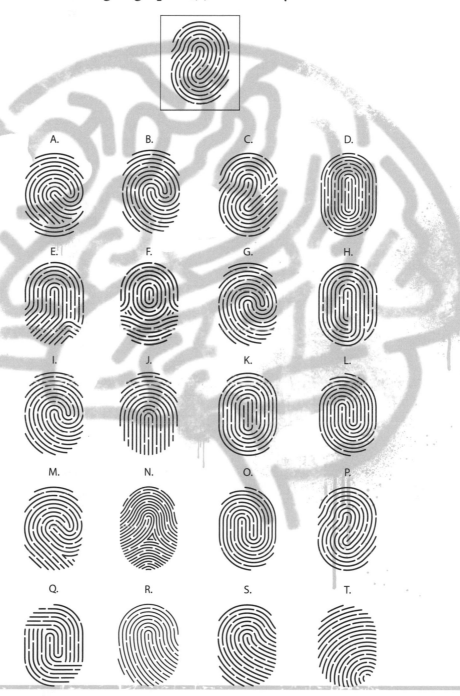

A.   B.   C.   D.

E.   F.   G.   H.

I.   J.   K.   L.

M.   N.   O.   P.

Q.   R.   S.   T.

Answers on page 188.

SHIPPING RATES

Five customers shipped items of varying weights and sizes, and you know evidence is found in one of them. The post office determines the shipping price of a parcel based on its weight and overall dimensions (shown as: length x width x height) as well as the package's final destination, speed of shipment, and inclusion of additional services, such as insurance and delivery confirmation. Using only the following clues, determine the size and weight of each customer's box, as well as the final price they were charged by the post office to ship it to its destination.

     1. Of Katrina's box and the largest package of the 5, one weighed 4.5 lbs and the other cost $27.09 to ship.

     2. The 12-inch wide package weighed more than the one that was most expensive to ship.

     3. The lightest of the 5 packages was, in terms of shape, a perfect cube.

     4. The 5 packages were the smallest one (which wasn't Mitch's), the second-lightest box, Tristan's (which didn't cost $29.67 to ship), the second-heaviest box, and the one that cost $27.09 to ship.

     5. The package that weighed 4.8 lbs belonged to neither Tristan nor Abigail.

     6. Of the 10-inch tall box and the one that was cheapest to ship, one belonged to Mitch and the other to Katrina.

     7. Abigail's package weighed a third of a pound less than the 8 x 10 x 8 box.

	Abigail	Charles	Katrina	Mitch	Tristan	6 x 8 x 8	8 x 10 x 8	8 x 12 x 12	10 x 10 x 10	12 x 16 x 12	$24.25	$26.53	$27.09	$29.67	$32.10
Weights 4.2 lbs															
4.5 lbs															
4.8 lbs															
5.1 lbs															
5.4 lbs															
Prices $24.25															
$26.53															
$27.09															
$29.67															
$32.10															
Dimensions 6 x 8 x 8															
8 x 10 x 8															
8 x 12 x 12															
10 x 10 x 10															
12 x 16 x 12															

Weights	Customers	Dimensions	Prices
4.2 lbs			
4.5 lbs			
4.8 lbs			
5.1 lbs			
5.4 lbs			

CRACK THE PASSWORD

The criminal left behind a list of scrambled passwords. This puzzle functions exactly like an anagram with an added step: In addition to being scrambled, each word below is missing the same letter. Discover the missing letter, then unscramble the words.

ORNATE

REKNIT

CARATE

INCREMENT

CRACK THE PASSWORD

The criminal left behind a list of scrambled passwords. This puzzle functions exactly like an anagram with an added step: In addition to being scrambled, each word below is missing the same letter. Discover the missing letter, then unscramble the words.

MATIER

BILLON

TODDLE

Answers on page 188.

SEEN AT THE SCENE PART I

Study this picture of the crime scene for 1 minute, then turn the page.

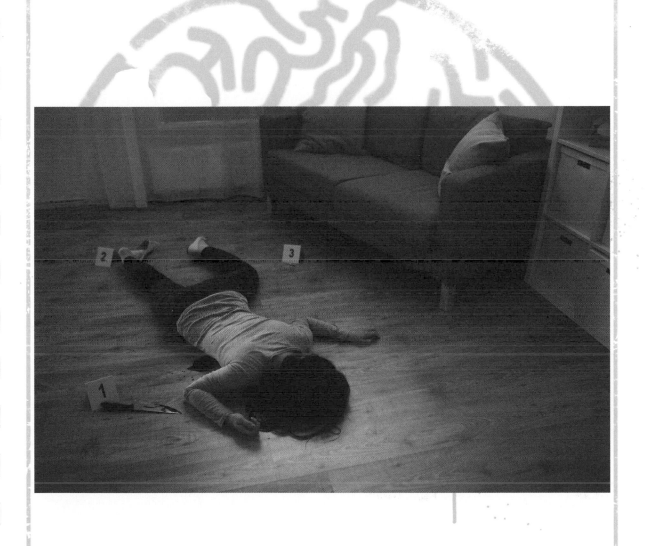

SEEN AT THE SCENE PART II

(Do not read this until you have read the previous page!)
Which image exactly matches the picture from the previous page?

1.

2.

3.

4.

Answers on page 188.

MOTEL HIDEOUT

A thief hides out in one of the 45 motel rooms listed in the chart below. The motel's in-house detective received a sheet of four clues, signed "The Logical Thief." Using these clues, the detective found the room number within 15 minutes—but by that time, the thief had fled. Can you find the thief's motel room more quickly?

1. **The number can be divided by 6.**

2. **The number cannot be divided by 4.**

3. **The sum of the digits is 8 or greater.**

4. **The second digit is greater than 6.**

51	52	53	54	55	56	57	58	59
41	42	43	44	45	46	47	48	49
31	32	33	34	35	36	37	38	39
21	22	23	24	25	26	27	28	29
11	12	13	14	15	16	17	18	19

Answers on page 189.

NAME THAT DETECTIVE

Cryptograms are messages in substitution code. Break the code to read the message. For example, THE SMART CAT might become FVO QWGDF JGF if **F** is substituted for **T**, **V** for **H**, **O** for **E**, and so on. Bonus question: Who is described in the quote? Which story is the source of the quote?

EFN FEMW SHL CBJ KTJLN-KMFFJ KMH TERHZBZ
HN HMM CFQJL PW NCJFEOL FK LTEOQMHJ HEZ
FKNBE QEZBLTJHPMB UCHJHUNBJL PQN CBJ
JBAHJYHPMB MFZOBJ LCFSBZ HE BUUBENJTUTNW
HEZ TJJBOQMHJTNW TE CTL MTKB SCTUC
AQLN CHRB LFJBMW NJTBZ CBJ GHNTBEUB. CTL
TEUJBZTPMB QENTZTEBLL, CTL HZZTUNTFE NF
AQLTU HN LNJHEOB CFQJL, CTL FUUHLTFEHM
JBRFMRBJ GJHUNTUB STNCTE ZFFJL, CTL SBTJZ HEZ
FKNBE AHMFZFJFQL LUTBENTKTU BVGBJTABENL,
HEZ NCB HNAFLGCBJB FK RTFMBEUB HEZ ZHEOBJ
SCTUC CQEO HJFQEZ CTA AHZB CTA NCB RBJW
SFJLN NBEHEN TE MFEZFE. FE NCB FNCBJ CHEZ, CTL
GHWABENL SBJB GJTEUBMW.

152

OVERHEARD INFORMATION PART I

Read the story below, then turn the page and answer the questions.

While on a train, a bystander overheard a conversation between two thieves about where some stolen goods were stashed. The woman said to her acccomplice, "I don't know where Kensington took his share, but he had the designer purses. I left the sapphire choker underneath the floorboard in the Lakeview condo, and the matching bracelet inside the base of that really ugly lamp in the living room, you know the one. Michaels got the jade figurine, and that fool is keeping it in his office, just out on a shelf. He says it's not recognizable. I have half a mind to steal it from him, just to keep it secure."

OVERHEARD INFORMATION PART II

(Do not read this until you have read the previous page!)

1. The location of these goods is unknown.
A. Choker
B. Bracelet
C. Figurine
D. Designer purses

2. Who does the speaker call a fool?
A. Kensington
B. Michaels
C. Herself
D. Her listener

3. The speaker's share of the stolen goods are kept here:
A. A house in Lakeside
B. A condo in Lakeview
C. An apartment in Lake Bluff
D. A cottage in Lakeland

4. The stolen figurine is made of this material.
A. Jade
B. Sapphire
C. Ivory
D. The material is not given.

Answers on page 189.

TREASURE HUNT

The investigator is tracking a jewelry thief's past trips in order to find and recover jewelry that was left behind in six cities. Each city was visited only once. Can you put together the travel timeline, using the information below?

1. The thief began and ended in different countries.

2. The trips to Salt Lake City and Pittsburgh were not back to back.

3. The thief flew immediately from San Antonio to Phoenix.

4. The thief visited Quebec sometime before Calgary.

5. The two cities that start with S were visited back to back, as were the two cities that start with P.

6. Phoenix was one of the first four cities visited.

UNDERCOVER STING

You know your quarry has reservations tonight at Coq au Vin, and you're trying to get the lay of the land. The restaurant prides itself on its service as well as its food, and it always makes sure that every table has its own dedicated waiter or waitress. Using the clues below and the charts on the next page, figure out the reservation time and party size for each of the next 5 tables to be seated this evening, as well as the name of the waiter or waitress who will be assigned to that table.

1. The 5 tables are the Elkin party (which won't be served by Parker), the largest and smallest parties, the one with the 6:15 P.M. reservation, and the table Audrey will be serving.

2. The Martinson party reserved a table for 6:30 P.M.

3. Between the Elkin party and the one with the 6:00 p.m. reservation, one requested a table for 3 and the other a table for 8.

4. The table Christopher will be serving (which isn't the Jackson party) has an earlier reservation than the party that requested a table for 2.

5. The five parties are the 6:15 P.M. reservation, the one that requested a table for 6 (which isn't the Jackson party), the latest of the 5 reservations, the Martinson party, and the one Stoya will be serving.

6. The Littleford party doesn't have the earliest reservation.

		Daniels	Elkin	Jackson	Littleford	Martinson	2	3	5	6	8	Audrey	Christopher	Parker	Stoya	Vanessa
Reservations	5:40 pm															
	6:00 pm															
	6:15 pm															
	6:30 pm															
	7:15 pm															
Servers	Audrey															
	Christopher															
	Parker															
	Stoya															
	Vanessa															
Party Sizes	2															
	3															
	5															
	6															
	8															

Reservations	Names	Party Sizes	Servers
5:40 pm			
6:00 pm			
6:15 pm			
6:30 pm			
7:15 pm			

Answers on page 189.

MOTEL HIDEOUT

A thief hides out in one of the 45 motel rooms listed in the chart below. The motel's in-house detective received a sheet of four clues, signed "The Logical Thief." Using these clues, the detective found the room number within 15 minutes—but by that time, the thief had fled. Can you find the thief's motel room more quickly?

1. **The sum of the digits is greater than 3 but less than 11.**

2. **The first digit is larger than the second.**

3. **One of the digits is 3.**

4. **The number is not prime.**

51	52	53	54	55	56	57	58	59
41	42	43	44	45	46	47	48	49
31	32	33	34	35	36	37	38	39
21	22	23	24	25	26	27	28	29
11	12	13	14	15	16	17	18	19

Answers on page 189.

WHAT CHANGED? PART I

Study this picture of the crime scene for 1 minute, then turn the page.

WHAT CHANGED? PART II

(Do not read this until you have read the previous page!)
From memory, can you tell what changed between this page and the previous page?

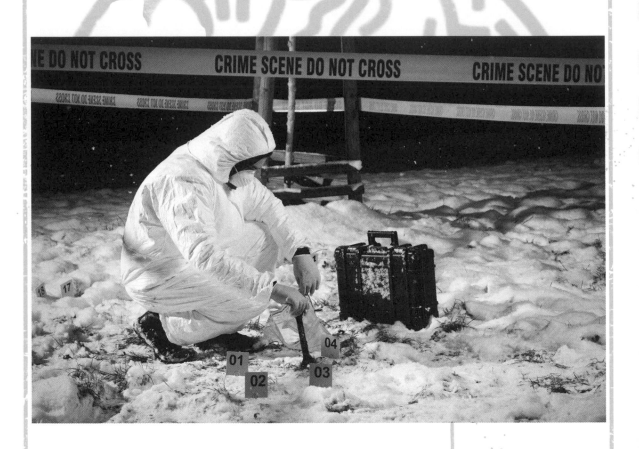

160

Answers on page 189.

OVERHEARD INFORMATION PART I

Read the story below, then turn the page and answer the questions.

A bystander heard two people talking at a coffee shop, only to realize they were counterfeiters! One said to the other, "The order is thirty-five $20 dollar bills, sixty $100 bills, and one hundred $10 bills. I've left it in the safe, and the temporary combination is 03-21-17. You need to pick it up by Thursday at 6 PM or the money is removed."

OVERHEARD INFORMATION PART II

(Do not read this until you have read the previous page!)

1. How many bills of each denomination are being delivered? (For some, the answer may be zero.)

$5: _____

$10: _____

$20: _____

$50: _____

$100: _____

2. What is the combination for the safe?

_____

3. What is the deadline to pick up the delivery?

_____

Answers on page 190.

INTERCEPTION

You've intercepted two messages between criminal masterminds. One informed you they would be meeting in a European city on a specific date. The other is the list of European cities seen below. The only problem is, the message shows many European cities, not just one. Can you figure out the right location?

PRAGUE

TALLINN

WARSAW

SOFIA

BRUSSELS

Answers on page 190.

TREASURE HUNT

The investigator is tracking a jewelry thief's past trips in order to find and recover jewelry that was left behind in six cities. Each city was visited only once. Can you put together the travel timeline, using the information below?

1. The two cities on the Mississippi River were visited back to back, as were the two cities on the Pacific Coastline. The two Canadian cities were not visited one after the other.

2. St. Louis was visited sometime before Ottawa, but sometime after Los Angeles.

3. San Francisco was one of the first three cities visited.

4. New Orleans was one of the last four cities visited.

5. Quebec was visited sometime before Ottawa, but after the West Coast cities.

6. Three cities were visited between Los Angeles and New Orleans.

164

Answers on page 190.

SEEN AT THE SCENE PART I

Study this picture of the crime scene for 1 minute, then turn the page.

SEEN AT THE SCENE PART II

(Do not read this until you have read the previous page!)

1. A wineglass is found on the floor.
_____ True
_____ False

2. Both investigators are wearing masks.
_____ True
_____ False

3. A chair had been knocked over.
_____ True
_____ False

4. A potted plant had been knocked over.
_____ True
_____ False

Answers on page 190.

MOTEL HIDEOUT

A thief hides out in one of the 45 motel rooms listed in the chart below. The motel's in-house detective received a sheet of four clues, signed "The Logical Thief." Using these clues, the detective found the room number within 15 minutes—but by that time, the thief had fled. Can you find the thief's motel room more quickly?

1. The sum of the digits is either less than 5 or greater than 9.

2. If you multiply one of the digits by 2, you get the second digit.

3. If you spell out the number, it is more than 6 letters.

4. The number is not divisible by 7.

51	52	53	54	55	56	57	58	59
41	42	43	44	45	46	47	48	49
31	32	33	34	35	36	37	38	39
21	22	23	24	25	26	27	28	29
11	12	13	14	15	16	17	18	19

Answers on page 190.

CRIME RHYMES

Each clue leads to a 2-word answer that rhymes, such as BIG PIG or STABLE TABLE. The numbers in parentheses after the clue give the number of letters in each word. For example, "cookware taken from the oven (3, 3)" would be "hot pot."

1. Murder amongst Neanderthals (10, 7): _____

2. Person who wants to be a PI (11, 9): _____

3. When the police officer likes to play hockey in spare time (6, 12): _____

4. An investigator who specializes in crimes involving dental work (5, 6): _____

5. A line of people waiting at the detective's door (7, 5): _____

6. The detective called the fingerprint found on the candy cane this (10, 5): _____

7. The local ornithological society was horrified when a member was killed in what was later called this (6, 6): _____

8. The case of the poison being found in the toothpaste was called this (8, 8): _____

Answers on page 190.

CRIME SCENE

Every word listed is contained within the group of letters. Words can be found in a straight line horizontally, vertically, or diagonally. They may be read either forward or backward.

CRIME

_____

_____

_____

_____ **a communication device**

_____

_____

_____

_____

_____ **not large**

_____

_____

_____ **a type of wheat**

_____

_____

SCENE

Bonus: Can you do this word ladder with only five words between CRIME and SCENE, using a Scottish verb meaning "shrivel" and a noun referring to a cut of meat that includes the backbone?

SUSPENSE NOVELS

ACROSS

1. "Better late than never" is one
6. Catches, as fly balls
11. Chuck who sang "Maybellene"
12. Fulcrum
13. Show's host
14. Bowl game setting
15. 2000 James Patterson's thriller
17. Copier powders
18. Actor De Niro
21. Ending with Juan or senor
24. Become worn away
25. Like Humpty Dumpty
27. "Runaway" rocker Shannon
28. Completely destroyed
29. Dimwits
32. 2003 Dan Brown blockbuster, with "The"
37. Non-earthling
38. Handrail post
39. Old Wells Fargo transport
40. Like the Parthenon
41. Show respect for
42. Bygone Vegas hotel

DOWN

1. But, to Brahms
2. Audition platter, for short
3. Arrow trajectories
4. Said hello to
5. Decrepit building, e.g.
6. "Donut" in a car trunk
7. Employer, often
8. Intense dislike
9. "___ Girl," 2012 psychological thriller by Gillian Flynn
10. Large town, in Dutch
16. Colony member
18. "___ Dragon," 1981 Thomas Harris suspense novel
19. Bauxite or magnetite
20. Sucre native
22. Make a granny knot
23. Calculate a total
25. Picnics, e.g.
26. Innards
28. Huge bird of myth
30. Mexican muralist Rivera
31. Exclusive, as a "circle"
32. A little bit of salt
33. A choir voice
34. John Irving's "A Prayer for ___ Meany"
35. Closing document
36. American wapitis

FINGERPRINT MATCH

Find the matching fingerprint(s). There may be more than one.

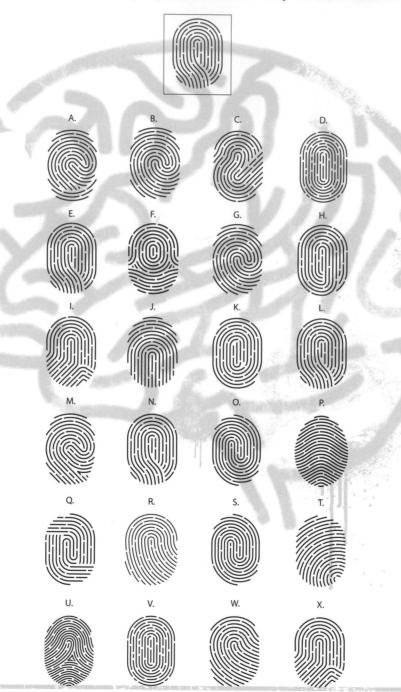

Answers on page 191.

SEEN AT THE SCENE PART I

Study this picture of the crime scene for 1 minute, then turn the page.

SEEN AT THE SCENE PART II

(Do not read this until you have read the previous page!)
Which image exactly matches the picture from the previous page?

1.

2.

3.

4.

Answers on page 191.

ANSWER PAGE

A FAMOUS CRIME (page 4)

1994 saw the theft of a version of Edvard Munch's painting The Scream from a gallery in Oslo. The thieves left behind a note thanking the museum for poor security. The last laugh was on the museum, though, as police recovered the painting and caught the thieves.

INTERCEPTION (page 4)

In each word, find the letter that occurs twice, and you end up with: Library, Monday

WHAT CHANGED? PART II (page 6)

A binder disappeared.

FIND THE WITNESS (page 7)

Chin lives in house D.

TEST THE ALIBI (page 8)

Brightly's alibi does have a gap between about 6:15 and 7:30 PM. She could have left her workplace around 6:15, gotten to Jones's house shortly after he himself arrived home, committed the murder, and returned to her workplace for the close of the function.

SEEN AT THE SCENE PART II (page 10)

Picture 4 is a match.

WEDDING BELL BLUES PART II (page 12)

1. D. 2005; 2. A. Operation Royal Charm; 3. B. $4.4 million; 4. C. Atlantic City

ANSWER PAGE

TREASURE HUNT (page 13)

The order is: Cleveland (Ohio, United States), Las Vegas (Nevada, United States), Toronto (Canada), Tulsa (Oklahoma, United States), Houston (Texas, United States), Mexico City (Mexico).

MOTEL HIDEOUT (page 14)

The thief is in room 41.

SEEN AT THE SCENE PART II (page 16)

Picture 4 is a match.

OVERHEARD INFORMATION PART II (page 18)

1. C. $5,000, which is an unspecified portion of what is found there; 2. Parkway; 3. B. August-Medicare-December; 4. A. A cedar chest

CRIME RHYMES (page 19)

1. might indict; 2. watermelon felon; 3. physician suspicion; 4. vermouth sleuth; 5. glue clue; 6. investigate the first mate; 7. lakeside homicide; 8. prospective detective

CRIME ON TV (page 20)

B	O	N	E	S		P	A	I	L	S
O	D	I	S	T		A	S	N	I	T
M	E	C	C	A		T	I	A	R	A
B	R	E	A	K	I	N	G	B	A	D
		P	I	S	A	N	O			
S	I	R	E	N	S		O	L	E	
Q	U	E	E	G		S	S	T	A	R
S	M	L		U	T	A	H	A	N	
		E	M	I	N	E	M			
S	E	A	R	C	H	P	A	R	T	Y
I	T	S	M	E		O	R	U	R	O
G	R	E	E	R		F	R	E	A	K
N	E	S	T	S		F	A	R	G	O

176

ANSWER PAGE

SPOTTING A CLUE (page 22)
Answers may vary. SPOT, slot, sloe, slue, CLUE

FORGING MONEY (page 22)
Answers may vary. FORGE, forte, forts, fores, bores, bones, hones, honey, MONEY

SEEN AT THE SCENE PART II (page 24)
Picture 3 is a match.

FIND THE WITNESS (page 25)
Boyd lives in house C.

INTERCEPTION (page 26)
Take the first and last letter of each word. The meeting will take place: Friday, noon, Atlanta

WE STILL DON'T KNOW WHO DONE IT (page 26)
One famous unsolved case involves thefts of artwork from the Isabella Stewart Gartner Museum. In 1990, men posing as police officers stole 13 works of art worth hundreds of millions of dollars. Empty frames at the museum show where the artwork was.

MOTEL HIDEOUT (page 27)
The thief is in room 11.

BOTCHED CRIME JOBS PART II (page 30)
1. A. Al Capone; 2. B. Gambinos; 3. C. Enrico Frigerio; 4. D. $700,000

ANSWER PAGE

SEEN AT THE SCENE PART II (page 32)
Picture 2 is a match.

TREASURE HUNT (page 33)
The order was: Dallas (Texas); Newark (New Jersey); Toronto (Ontario); Albany (New York); Los Angeles (California), and Madison (Wisconsin). The states of Wisconsin and New York, and the province of Ontario, all border a Great Lake.

FINGERPRINT MATCH (page 34)
F is the matching fingerprint.

OVERHEARD INFORMATION PART II (page 36)
1. B. The 21st; 2. D. A location is not given. 3. B. False; 4. C. Diner

SEEN AT THE SCENE PART II (page 38)
Picture 2 is a match.

GOING UNDERCOVER PART II (page 40)
1. D. Wade; 2. C. Wanda; 3. A. TJ; 4. A. Three months

CRIME RHYMES (page 41)
1. stolen colon; 2. yuletide homicide; 3. subliminal criminal; 4. indict knight; 5. swaps cops; 6. steal oatmeal; 7. illegal beagle; 8. mime crime

NOTORIOUS ART THEFTS PART II (page 44)
1. B. The Louvre; 2. C. A motorboat; 3. A. Police officers; 4. False

ANSWER PAGE

WHAT CHANGED? PART II (page 46)
A jar disappeared.

SEEN AT THE SCENE PART II (page 48)
Picture 3 is a match.

FIND THE WITNESS (page 49)
Williams live in house C.

INTERCEPTION (page 50)
Take the first two letters of each place name: The meet will take place on East Washington Street at the diner at 7 AM.

OVERHEARD INFORMATION PART II (page 52)
1. C. Gems and dollhouse; 2. B. 2004; 3. A. At least two; 4. C. East

SEEN AT THE SCENE PART II (page 54)
Picture 1 is a match.

TREASURE HUNT (page 55)
The order is: Reno (Nevada, United States), Philadelphia (Pennsylvania, United States), Miami (Florida, United States), Lima (Peru), Vancouver (Canada), Cabo San Lucas (Mexico)

MOTEL HIDEOUT (page 56)
The thief is in room 23.

ANSWER PAGE

JAIL CELLS (page 57)
Answers may vary. JAIL, fail, fall, fell, CELL

FLEEING THE SCENE (page 57)
Answers may vary. FLEES, fleet, sleet, sheet, shent, scent, SCENE

TRACK THE CRIMINAL (page 58)

	City	Number
1.	Miami	33
2.	Chicago	45
3.	New York	45
4.	Dallas	25
5.	Atlanta	63
6.	Denver	58
7.	Los Angeles	87
8.	Phoenix	32
9.	Seattle	
	TOTAL	388

WHAT WENT MISSING? PART II (page 60)
All the books on the top right shelf have gone missing. The documents were hidden in one of them.

SEEN AT THE SCENE PART II (page 62)
Picture 3 is a match.

OVERHEARD INFORMATION PART II (page 64)
1. A. A bakery; 2. A. February 8; 3. A. February 8. The theft will only be delayed if it snows; 4. D. Fourth

ANSWER PAGE

MOTEL HIDEOUT (page 65)
The thief is in room 49.

TREASURE HUNT (page 66)
The order is: Baltimore, Los Angeles, Toronto, Seattle, Atlanta, Detroit.

SEEN AT THE SCENE PART II (page 68)
Picture 1 is a match.

FIND THE WITNESS (page 69)
The Wests live in house D.

INTERCEPTION (page 70)
Take the first letter of the first word, the last letter of the second word, the first letter of the third word, and the last letter of the fourth word. Continue, alternating between the first letter of one word and the final letter of the next word, until you have the whole message: Cottage Grove Inn, Room Eight

TREASURE HUNT (page 71)
The order is: Nashville (United States); Seoul (South Korea); Buenos Aires (Argentina); Athens (Greece); Denver (United States); Atlanta (United States)

CRIME RHYMES (page 72)
1. parson arson; 2. vase case; 3. flint print; 4. reef thief; 5. skyscraper caper; 6. herder murder; 7. steal glockenspiel; 8. iced heist

WHAT WENT MISSING? PART II (page 74)
The cotton swabs went missing.

ANSWER PAGE

OVERHEARD INFORMATION PART II (page 76)
1. D. The CTO; 2. C. East; 3. B. In the CEO's office, behind the abstract painting; 4. A. 87-35-14

THE COUNTERFEIT HOUSE PART II (page 78)
1. C. 50-cent; 2. C. Seven; 3. A. Two; 4. False

SEEN AT THE SCENE PART II (page 80)
Picture 1 is a match.

MOTEL HIDEOUT (page 81)
The thief is in room 21.

A MASTER FORGER PART II (page 84)
1. D. Drewe's ex-wife; 2. True; 3. A. 10%; 4. False. He served four months.

FIRST STEAL, THEN FLEE (page 85)
Answers may vary. STEAL, steel, steep, sleep, sleet, fleet, FLEES

WILL A PLOT LEAD TO JAIL? (page 85)
Answers may vary. PLOT, slot, slit, slid, said, sail, JAIL

FINGERPRINT MATCH (page 86)
A and L are the matching fingerprints.

SEEN AT THE SCENE PART II (page 88)
Picture 4 is a match.

ANSWER PAGE

FIND THE WITNESS (page 89)
Shah lives in house A.

TREASURE HUNT (page 90)
The order is: Memphis (United States), Acapulco (Mexico), Edmonton (Canada), Panama City (Panama), Portland (United States), Phoenix (United States)

INTERCEPTION (page 91)
Take the central letter of each place name and the result is BERLIN.

MOTEL HIDEOUT (page 92)
The thief is in room 54.

OVERHEARD INFORMATION PART II (page 94)
1. D. None of the above; 2. B. The CFO and his assistant; 3. C. 21-45-93; 4. A. An unspecified payment

WHAT CHANGED? PART II (page 96)
An evidence sheet disappeared.

SEEN AT THE SCENE PART II (page 98)
Picture 2 is a match.

NOTHING TO DO WITH DOYLE (page 99)
H.H. Holmes wasn't a fictional detective—he was a serial killer, often considered the first in America. Born Herman Webster Mudgett in 1861, he confessed to 27 murders but may have been responsible for more. He was also a bigamist, married to three women at the time of his death.

ANSWER PAGE

VALACHI SPEAKS PART II (page 102)
1. C. Omerta; 2. C. $100,000; 3. A. Senate Permanent Investigations Subcommittee; 4. C. 1968

OVERHEARD INFORMATION PART II (page 104)
1. A. The first floor at Rivers Edgetown Mall; 2. D. Electronics store; 3. C. Butterlake Drive; 4. B. June 10

SEEN AT THE SCENE PART II (page 106)
Picture 2 is a match.

FIND THE WITNESS (page 107)
Ramirez lives in house A.

INTERCEPTION (page 108)
Take the last letter of each place name to reveal: Kansas City

TREASURE HUNT (page 109)
The order is: Vancouver, San Diego, Rio de Janeiro, Chicago, Boston, Calgary

MOTEL HIDEOUT (page 110)
The thief is in room 56.

OVERHEARD INFORMATION PART II (page 112)
1. Matty; 2. I've met your cousin Louise, isn't she the best?; 3. Monday, Wednesday, and Friday; 4. Waverly Place

SEEN AT THE SCENE PART II (page 114)
Picture 3 is a match.

ANSWER PAGE

LEAVING CLUES (page 115)

Answers may vary. LEAVE, lease, cease, chase, chasm, charm, chars, chaps, chips, clips, flips, flies, flues, CLUES

CRIME SCENE (page 116)

¹S	²T	³A	⁴I	⁵R		⁶S	⁷P	⁸O	⁹R	¹⁰T

(crossword solution grid)

S	T	A	I	R	■	S	P	O	R	T
O	U	I	D	A	■	A	R	M	O	R
D	N	A	E	V	I	D	E	N	C	E
■	■	E	A	R	L	■	E	S	E	■
A	H	A	■	G	O	Y	A	■	■	■
L	A	W	M	E	N	■	M	I	N	T
B	L	O	O	D	■	F	I	B	E	R
S	O	L	D	■	M	E	D	I	C	O
■	■	E	G	A	D	■	S	K	Y	■
I	T	S	■	O	R	E	S	■	■	■
P	H	O	T	O	G	R	A	P	H	S
S	E	R	I	F	■	A	R	E	A	S
E	N	E	M	Y	■	L	A	R	G	E

FINGERPRINT MATCH (page 118)

E is the matching fingerprint.

CRACK THE PASSWORD (page 119)

The missing letter is E.
BROMIDE
CODEINE
RETAINER
ELEVATE

CRACK THE PASSWORD (page 119)

The missing letter is E.
ENDEMIC
GARBAGE
GEOLOGY
GOUACHE

ANSWER PAGE

MOTEL HIDEOUT (page 120)
The thief is in room 59.

WHAT CHANGED? PART II (page 122)
The envelope near the investigator's hand has disappeared.

FIND THE WITNESS (page 123)
Beal lives in house E.

INTERCEPTION (page 124)
Take the central letter of each word and you get NILBUD. Flip this, and it becomes DUBLIN.

TREASURE HUNT (page 125)
The order is: Minneapolis (Minnesota); Winnipeg (Canada); Orlando (Florida); Guadalajara (Mexico); Seattle (Washington); Washington, D.C.

CRIME RHYMES (page 126)
1. deft theft; 2. pie alibi; 3. admire fire; 4. collect suspect; 5. bitter counterfeiter; 6. tollbooth sleuth; 7. maritime crime; 8. jackplot plot

OVERHEARD INFORMATION PART II (page 128)
West side: "Do you know if the salad dressing has MSG?" Downtown: "Do you have the zucchini lasagna on the menu tonight?" Near north: "You have the most delicious brownies for dessert, pass my compliments to the chef!" East side: "Is Lon in the kitchen tonight? He makes the best burgers."

SEEN AT THE SCENE PART II (page 130)
1. Knife; 2. Open; 3. False; 4. True

ANSWER PAGE

TEST THE ALIBI (page 131)

Smith's alibi has a gap of time when he is not accounted for. Tina places the card game as ending around 10:30, and his friend T.R. around 11 PM. From that point until the bartender shows a credit card receipt at 12:30 AM, Smith has no one who can place him definitively at the party.

MAFIA BUSTER PART II (page 134)

1. Captain Alexander Williams; 2. Vito Cascio Ferro; 3. Police Commissioner Theodore Bingham; 4. Beggar, laborer, merchant Simone Velletri

MOTEL HIDEOUT (page 135)

The thief is in room 15.

A LONG PATH FROM CRIME TO TRIAL (page 136)

Answers may vary. CRIME, grime, gripe, grips, grins, gains, pains, pairs, hairs, hairy, dairy, daily, drily, drill, trill, TRIAL

OVERHEARD INFORMATION PART II (page 138)

1. A. Two men; 2. D. 05-36-29; 3. B. Thursday; 4. B. Kerri

WHAT CHANGED? PART II (page 140)

The gun moved closer to card 2.

SEEN AT THE SCENE PART II (page 142)

Picture 1 is a match.

FIND THE WITNESS (page 143)

The Stovens are in house C.

ANSWER PAGE

INTERCEPTION (page 144)
Take the second letter of each word to reveal: Barcelona

FINGERPRINT MATCH (page 145)
P is the matching fingerprint.

SHIPPING RATES (page 146)

Weights	Customers	Dimensions	Prices
4.2 lbs	Katrina	10 x 10 x 10	$27.09
4.5 lbs	Mitch	12 x 16 x 12	$24.25
4.8 lbs	Charles	6 x 8 x 8	$32.10
5.1 lbs	Abigail	8 x 12 x 12	$29.67
5.4 lbs	Tristan	8 x 10 x 8	$26.53

CRACK THE PASSWORD (page 148)
The missing letter is H.
ANOTHER
THINKER
TRACHEA
ENRICHMENT

CRACK THE PASSWORD (page 148)
The missing letter is I.
AIRTIME
BILLION
DELTOID

SEEN AT THE SCENE PART II (page 150)
Picture 2 is a match.

ANSWER PAGE

MOTEL HIDEOUT (page 151)
The thief is in room 18.

NAME THAT DETECTIVE (page 152)
Not only was her first-floor flat invaded at all hours by throngs of singular and often undesirable characters but her remarkable lodger showed an eccentricity and irregularity in his life which must have sorely tried her patience. His incredible untidiness, his addiction to music at strange hours, his occasional revolver practice within doors, his weird and often malodorous scientific experiments, and the atmosphere of violence and danger which hung around him made him the very worst tenant in London. On the other hand, his payments were princely.

Bonus answer: Mrs. Hudson and Sherlock Holmes are described in "The Adventure of the Dying Detective"

OVERHEARD INFORMATION PART II (page 154)
1. D. Designer purses; 2. B. Michaels; 3. B. A condo in Lakeview; 4. A. Jade

TREASURE HUNT (page 155)
The order is: Salt Lake City (United States), San Antonio (United States), Phoenix (United States), Pittsburgh (United States), Quebec (Canada), Calgary (Canada)

UNDERCOVER STING (page 156)

Reservations	Names	Party Sizes	Servers
5:40 pm	Daniels	6	Audrey
6:00 pm	Jackson	8	Stoya
6:15 pm	Littleford	5	Christopher
6:30 pm	Martinson	2	Parker
7:15 pm	Elkin	3	Vanessa

MOTEL HIDEOUT (page 158)
The thief is in room 32.

WHAT CHANGED? PART II (page 160)
Evidence markers 8, 9, and 10 have disappeared from the scene.

ANSWER PAGE

OVERHEARD INFORMATION PART II (page 162)
1. Zero $5 bills, 100 $10 bills, 35 $20 bills, zero $50 bills, 60 $100 bills
2. 03-21-17
3. Thursday at 6 PM

INTERCEPTION (page 163)
Take the first letter of the first word, the second letter of the second word, the third letter of the third word, the fourth letter of the fourth word, and the fifth letter of the fifth word to reveal that the meeting will be held in PARIS.

TREASURE HUNT (page 164)
The order is: Los Angeles, San Francisco, Quebec, St. Louis, New Orleans, Ottawa

SEEN AT THE SCENE PART II (page 166)
1. True; 2. False; 3. False; 4. True

MOTEL HIDEOUT (page 167)
The thief is in room 48.

CRIME RHYMES (page 168)
1. prehistory mystery; 2. prospective detective; 3. skater investigator; 4. tooth sleuth; 5. gumshoe queue; 6. peppermint print; 7. birder murder; 8. fluoride homicide

CRIME SCENE (page 169)
Answers may vary. CRIME, prime, prise, prose, prone, phone, shone, stone, stole, stale, stall, small, smell, spell, spelt, spent, scent, SCENE. Variation: CRIME, crine, chine, shine, shone, scone, SCENE

ANSWER PAGE

SUSPENSE NOVELS (page 170)

A	D	A	G	E		S	H	A	G	S
B	E	R	R	Y		P	I	V	O	T
E	M	C	E	E		A	R	E	N	A
R	O	S	E	S	A	R	E	R	E	D
		T	O	N	E	R	S			
R	O	B	E	R	T			I	T	A
E	R	O	D	E		O	V	O	I	D
D	E	L		R	U	I	N	E	D	
	I	D	I	O	T	S				
D	A	V	I	N	C	I	C	O	D	E
A	L	I	E	N		N	E	W	E	L
S	T	A	G	E		G	R	E	E	K
H	O	N	O	R		S	A	N	D	S

FINGERPRINT MATCH (page 172)

E, L, and N are the matching fingerprints.

SEEN AT THE SCENE PART II (page 174)

Picture 1 is a match.